'*Pick Your Brains* children's travel guides for 8-12-year-olds stimulate children's interest in holiday destinations without being heavy handed … Plenty of fascinating facts presented with the kind of irreverence kids love.' *The Times*

'Any family heading abroad could do far worse than pack a copy of the excellent *Pick Your Brains About* travel guide series for children. Excellently designed, each one is written with the benefit of a twelve-year-old "guest editor" to keep the authors clued in to the facts and sights that will intrigue a young reader and drive adults mad with their questions.' Dermot Bolger, *Dublin Evening Herald*

'Let your child impress poolside companions and dinner guests on your costa holiday by spouting amusing anecdotes and informative tidbits about Spanish life and society, all harvested from this jolly piece of literature. Not a guidebook in the traditional sense, the series helps kids explore the culture and history of the country they are visiting with entertaining stories behind local customs, festivals and food.' [*Pick Your Brains About Spain*], Gemma Bowes, *Observer*

'A new travel guide for kids will keep little minds occupied for hours … *Pick Your Brains*, is a fun fact-filled series … the perfect antidote to plane/train/automobile rage.' *Irish Independent*

'some of this is fascinating and delivered in the sort of language many children will like.' [*Pick Your Brains About Italy*], Books of the Week, *Sunday Times*

'*Pick Your Brains About England*, an alternative tourist guide for eight to twelve-year-olds, is one of four books that explain the history of European countries in a light but informative way.' *Irish Times*

'A handy guide to great places to visit… Some of the places sound fab and you would never have heard about without a guidebook… it's all really clear and a cracking read.' ★★★★ review of the series, *Newsround website*, BBC 1

'*Pick Your Brains About England* will help bookworms swot up on their knowledge of England. There are cartoons and plenty of info on attractions, food and sport.' *Daily Express*

'These books tell you all about France, Spain, England and Italy…
Did you know that the Italians have a festival of chocolate or that
the Spanish throw tomatoes at each other? And as for the English,
did you know someone once tried to eat every animal known to
man?' *Blue Peter* website, *BBC 1*

'A fun new children's travel book *Pick Your Brains about England* has
the answers … and apart from fascinating facts, tells you the best
places to visit.' *The People*

'Curious kids? If you need quick answers to holiday questions from
inquisitive eight to twelve-year-olds, take a look at *Pick Your Brains
About* … packed with puzzles, facts and figures.' *Sainsbury's
Magazine*

'This new book series for kids lifts the lid on various holiday
destinations, including Italy, France, England and this one, Spain.
It's an involving introduction to España with sections of various
sights, festivals, history, phrases and customs … it's very readable.
Olé!' *Funday Times, Sunday Times*

'Canny publishers have come up with fun and easily accessible
guidebooks aimed exclusively at children – not a bad idea when
you consider children often choose the family holiday … a witty
series.' Chloë Bryan-Brown, *The Times* (Travel)

'*Pick Your Brains* is a fantastically fun travel series … It introduces
the cultures and customs of four European countries through their
food, history, landmarks, famous figures and recommends the very
best places to visit.' *Quiz Kids*

'For more fun facts about Spain, pick up the children's travel guide
series *Pick Your Brains About…*' *easyJet Magazine*

The Pick Your Brains series

England by Leo Hollis • *France* by Marian Pashley • *Ireland* by Mary
O'Neill • *Italy* by Jez Mathews • *Scotland* by Mandy Kirkby • *Spain* by
Mandy Kirkby • *USA* by Jane Egginton

PICK YOUR BRAINS

about

GREECE

Caroline Sanderson

Illustrations by
Caspar Williams & Craig Dixon

CADOGAN

Acknowledgements

The author and the publisher would like to thank 'guest editors' Beth, Felix
and Ella Fiducia-Brookes (all aged 11).

Published by Cadogan Guides 2005
Copyright © Caroline Sanderson 2005

Illustrations by Caspar Williams and Craig Dixon
Illustrations and map copyright © Cadogan Guides 2005
Map by (TW)

Cadogan Guides
Network House, 1 Ariel Way, London W12 7SL
info@cadoganguides.co.uk
www.cadoganguides.com

The Globe Pequot Press
246 Goose Lane, PO Box 480, Guilford,
Connecticut 06437–0480

Design and typesetting by Mathew Lyons
Printed in Italy by Legoprint

A catalogue record for this book is available
from the British Library
ISBN 1-86011-220-x

Contents

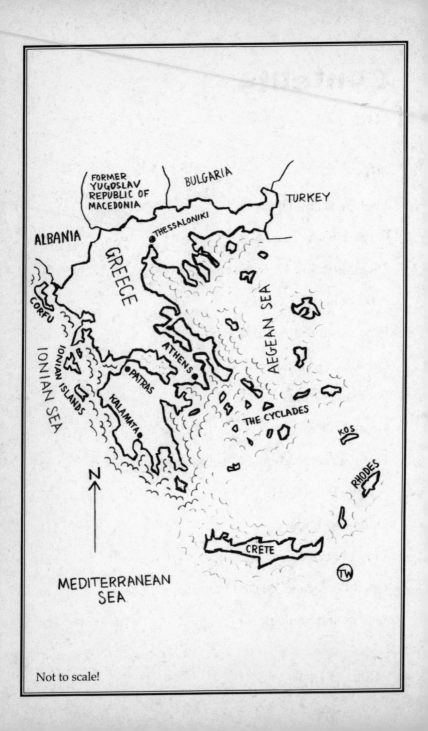

Not to scale!

Vital Facts
and Figures

Greece is a small but incredibly varied and beautiful country in southeastern Europe. It was home to one of the greatest of early civilisations, and so it has a rich and ancient history to go with its gorgeous beaches, its sun-drenched islands, and its friendly and lively people. Greece is stuffed full of interesting sights to see, and boasts a sunny and warm climate for most of the year, so it's the perfect place for a holiday.

The name 'Greece' comes from the Latin word *Graecia*, which is what the Romans called it. The Greeks call their country *Hellas*, or Ελλάδα in Greek letters.

Area: Greece is just a little bit bigger than England, at 131,957 square km (50,949 square miles).

Borders: Greece has land borders with four other countries: Albania, Former Yugoslav Republic of Macedonia, Bulgaria and Turkey.

Distances: It's 1,500 miles from London to Athens, the capital of Greece; it's 1,760 miles from Edinburgh to Athens and 1,780 miles from Dublin to Athens.

Population: There are around 11 million people in Greece. As recently as the 1960s well over half of Greece's population lived in the countryside. Now more than two thirds of them live in cities and towns.

Greece also has one of the highest relative populations of elderly people in the world, because on average people here

live longer than almost anywhere else (including the UK, Ireland and the US)!

Capital city: Athens, which has a population of 3.2 million

Other major cities (by population): Thessaloníki (or Salonika) 800,000; Pátras 174,000; Heráklion 135,000; Lárissa 133,000.

Currency: The euro replaced the old Greek currency, the drachma, on 1 January 2002. The drachma was the oldest currency in Europe.

Flag: The Greek national flag has nine horizontal blue and white stripes, and a white Greek cross on a blue background in the top left corner.

Time difference: Greece is two hours ahead of the UK.

Internet domain: The domain abbreviation for Greece is gr.

Geography: Greece is Europe's southernmost country, and lies at the end of the Balkan peninsula, which juts out into the Mediterranean Sea. It is a country of very varied landscape and climate, with one of the longest coastlines in Europe and many islands. Some of these, including Corfu, are on the western side of the mainland, in the Ionian Sea, but most are on its eastern side, in the Aegean Sea.

Greece lies on several fault lines in the earth's crust, so earth tremors are quite common. In 1986 the town of Kalamáta and the villages surrounding it in the south of Greece were devastated by a strong earthquake, which left more than 12,000 people homeless, especially as many houses were poorly built and collapsed easily. The Greek army is trained to provide emergency shelter, water and food supplies after earthquakes.

The highest point in Greece is Mount Olympus, 2,904m (9,570 feet) high, which the ancient Greeks believed was the home of the gods.

The longest river is the Aliakmon (297km).

Islands: Greece has more islands than any other country in Europe: more than 2,000, though only about 170 of them are inhabited. Crete is the largest Greek island, followed by Évia and Lésbos. Although the islands are among the most visited parts of Greece, they form only around 10 per cent of the country's total land area, so there are plenty of other places to see!

Climate: Most postcards you'll see of Greece show sandy beaches, blue seas and warm sunshine, and much of the country does enjoy hot, dry summers and mild winters. However, because three-quarters of the country is mountainous, in many places winter can be very cold and wet.

Language: Greek is the oldest spoken language in Europe; it's at least 4,000 years old. Modern Greek, or *demotikí*, the language spoken by Greeks today, developed from Classical or Ancient Greek. The difference between them is a bit like the difference between modern English and the English used by Chaucer or Shakespeare. But an even more ancient version of the language called *katharévousa* (which means

Greek has its own alphabet of 24 letters. It might seem a bit daunting to learn a whole new alphabet, but it's well worth trying to learn even a few letters, so that you can have a go at reading signs and labels when you are in Greece.

capital	small letter	called	sounds like
Α	α	álfa	a, as in father
Β	β	víta	v
Γ	γ	gámma	g or y sound
Δ	δ	délta	th as in though
Ε	ε	épsilon	e as in bet
Ζ	ζ	zíta	z
Η	η	íta	i as in ski
Θ	θ	thíta	th as in thin
Ι	ι	yóta	i as in ski
Κ	κ	káppa	k
Λ	λ	lámtha	l
Μ	μ	mi	m
Ν	ν	ni	n
Ξ	ξ	ksi	x as in ox
Ο	ο	ómicron	o as in toad
Π	π	pi	p
Ρ	ρ	ro	r
Σ	σ or ς	sígma	s
Τ	τ	taf	t
Υ	υ	ípsilon	y as in barely
Φ	φ	fi	f
Χ	χ	chi	ch as in loch
Ψ	ψ	psi	ps as in lips
Ω	ω	oméga	o as in toad

'clean language'!) can still be found on some shop signs and official forms.

Government: The official name for Greece is the Hellenic Republic. Greece became a republic in 1974. The head of state is the President. The Prime Minister and his Cabinet lead the Greek Parliament.

Greece is divided into nine large regions: Macedonia (not to be confused with the neighbouring country of the Former Yugoslav Republic of Macedonia!); Thrace; Épirus; Thessaly; Stereá Elláda (Central Greece) and Euboea; the Peloponnese; the Ionian Islands; the Aegean Islands; and Crete.

Getting around: Greek Railways (OSE) are quite slow and old-fashioned. Most people use the bus service (KTEL) to travel long distances, because the buses are regular, efficient and very cheap, and because there are few railways.

With so many islands, ferries

are also an important way of getting around both for Greeks and for tourists. The main ferry port is Piraeus, close to Athens. From here ferries, hydrofoils and catamarans leave for every part of the Aegean Sea and beyond. If you're visiting Athens, there is a Metro system.

On the roads, Greeks drive on the right, but not always very carefully! Motorcycles and scooters are also a very popular way of getting about. Because of the often very loud noise they make, the Greeks nickname their scooters *papákia* or 'little ducks'!

Religions: Nearly all Greeks (98 per cent) are loyal to Greek Orthodoxy, a form of Christianity. The Orthodox Church still holds a very important place in Greek society, even though the number of people who go to church has fallen over the past 30 years. Nearly every Greek person takes part in religious rituals and feast days. Easter and the Assumption of the Virgin on 15 August are the most important festivals, and are celebrated in every part of Greece.

Main industries and exports: Traditionally the Greek economy was based on agriculture, with many farmers living off their own produce: milk, yoghurt and meat from sheep and goats, wine from vines, and olive oil from olive trees. Greece is still an important producer of olive oil, olives, citrus fruit (including oranges and lemons), corn, wheat, cotton, rice and grapes.

Many Greeks also made their living from fishing, but these days, with the number of fish in the sea falling, many fishermen are finding it harder to earn their living in this way.

Greece is rich in natural minerals. It has large reserves of bauxite, a mineral that is used to make aluminium. Marble has been quarried in Greece since ancient times and is still widely used as a building material today. Did you know that Greece is also the second largest producer of cement in the world after China?

Today, one of Greece's most important industries is: tourism! There are over 12 million foreign visitors to Greece every single year, most of them in the summer months.

Opening hours: Official shopping hours in Greece are: Monday and Wednesday 9 am – 3 pm; Tuesday, Thursday and Friday 9 am – 7 pm; Saturday 8.30 am – 3.30 pm. Shops are usually closed on Sundays. In tourist areas, however, some shops stay open late into the evenings. Banks open from 8.20 am to 2 pm on Mondays to Thursdays, and from 8 am to 1.30 pm on Fridays. Big museums are usually open every day, with shorter opening hours in the winter, but some are closed on Mondays.

Greek History in a Nutshell

Greece has one of the oldest and most famous civilisations in the world, and its history goes back more than 5,000 years.

Prehistoric Greece

The first human settlements in Greece probably date back to around 6000 BC. They were peaceful farming communities. The simple way of life of these Pre-Hellenic people, as they are called, soon changed as they began trading with other lands and peoples.

Between 2000 and 1100 BC there were several important regional powers in Greece, which grew wealthy and powerful through seafaring and trading with other countries around the Mediterranean. Huge royal palaces were built. Two of the most famous are Knossos, on the island of Crete, and Mycenae, in the Peloponnese. Their ruins can still be seen today.

Crete was a very important trading place at this time and

the centre of Minoan culture. (This is the name that was given to the culture in the 20th century: it comes from the mythical King Minos of Crete, the son of Zeus and Europa.) The palace at Knossos survived two earthquakes, as well as a massive volcanic eruption on the island of Thíra (now called Santoríni) some time between 1500 and 1450 BC. Archaeologists have dug up many beautiful objects on Crete, including pottery with distinctive red and white designs on a dark background. The Minoans controlled the seas around Greece for around 800 years. When Knossos finally collapsed, Mycenae took over as the leading power in Greece, until it too fell, in around 1200 BC.

You can see Prehistoric Greece:

☞ on Crete, where the remains of the great Minoan royal palace at Knossos have been excavated, and many of its rooms have been restored to show what they might have looked like.

☞ at Mycenae in the Peloponnese, where you can see the ancient royal citadel of the Mycenaean civilisation, with its famous gate guarded by two beautifully carved stone lions (though, unfortunately, their heads are missing).

Many of the Greek myths and legends that we can read about in the works of writers such as Homer come from this time, featuring such famous names as Agamemnon and Odysseus. The stories show us that there was a lot of rivalry among these early Greek civilisations and many wars were fought over trading routes. The most powerful regions were those on the coasts, because they traded goods such as olives and minerals by sea. Greek settlements and city states could be found as far away as France, Spain and North Africa. The famous Greek writer Homer once said that the Greeks 'lived round the Mediterranean like frogs round a pond'.

The Trojan War, 1194–1184 BC

The Trojan War united the whole of Greece against the city of Troy (in what is now Turkey). According to legend, it was fought over a woman: Helen, the wife of Menelaus, King of Sparta. Helen fell in love with a man called Paris, who just happened to be a son of the King of Troy. Paris sailed over to Sparta and took Helen away to Troy with him. Furious,

Menelaus and his brother, King Agamemnon of Mycenae, laid siege to Troy for ten long years without success. Then the Greeks hit on a cunning plan: they pretended to sail away, but left behind them a large hollow wooden horse with soldiers hidden inside. The Trojans dragged the horse inside the city. Under cover of darkness the Greek soldiers crept out of the horse and opened the gates of the city, letting in the rest of the Greek army, which then killed all the men of Troy, enslaved all the women and children, and finally burned the city to the ground. The story of the Trojan War is told in Homer's famous poem *The Iliad*.

In reality, the Trojan War was probably about more than a jealous husband. Troy lay at the entrance to the Black Sea, and all Greece's corn had to travel by boat through its waters. The Trojans had been interfering with Greece's food supplies, so that's probably the real reason the Greeks got shirty with them.

It was about this time that the Greek alphabet first appeared in a form that is still recognisable in the modern alphabet in use today in Greece.

Classical Greece

The 9th century BC brought the first Greek 'city states'. Their word for 'city state' was *polis* (from which we get our English word 'politics').

21

These city states were run not just by kings and aristocrats but also by other important citizens. Each city state had its own special character, and the two most powerful were Athens and Sparta, which were to become bitter rivals over the following five centuries.

The city state of Sparta was situated in the southern Peloponnese. It was ruled by two kings, whose most important job was to be military commanders, and a class of warriors known as the Spartiates. The most important thing a man could do in Sparta was to become a good fighter. Every newborn baby was brought before a state committee, and if it was judged a weakling, it was thrown from a cliff! Boys left home to be trained to fight from the age of seven until they were about 30. They often had to endure quite horrid conditions, which is where we get our word 'spartan'. Girls, too, were trained to sprint and wrestle. Sparta needed a big army because it was almost always at war with its trading rivals and its people owned many slaves. For centuries it was the strongest military power in Greece.

The rival city state of Athens is usually thought of as a much more cultured place, home to famous writers such as Sophocles and Aristophanes, and philosophers including Socrates and Plato, whose works are still read and performed to this day. The civilisation of Athens was at its height around 500 BC, when it produced some of the world's greatest artists, dramatists, politicians, philosophers, mathematicians, doctors and scientists.

At this time Athens became the world's first ever democracy, a word that we get from the Greek *demokratía*, which means 'rule by the people'. Every free man was able to vote to choose who they wanted to represent them in government (but women, slaves and foreigners could not vote).

Every city state had an *acropolis* (meaning high town), which was both a fortress and a centre for religious worship. In Athens the acropolis included the temple of the Parthenon, still Athens's most important landmark 2,500 years later.

Although it wasn't as warlike a place as Sparta, Athens had a powerful army and navy too. It fought off the invading armies of the Persian king Darius, and then his successor Xerxes, in two famous battles, one on land, at

Marathon in 490 BC, and the other at sea, at Salamis in 480 BC. In a rare moment of unity, Athens got together with Sparta and other Greek city states, and they finally defeated the Persian army in 479 BC.

Athens and Sparta weren't friends for long! Between 431 and 404 BC they fought each other again in the Peloponnesian Wars. Though Sparta is usually said to have won, after this time both city states became less powerful.

Alexander the Great

One of the reasons for the decline of the city states was the growth of a new and powerful empire in Macedonia, in northern Greece, which had always been thought of as a bit remote and uncivilised. The Macedonian king, Philip II, who reigned from 359 to 336 BC, conquered Thrace in the northwest of Greece and then pushed southwards, eventually taking control of Athens and southern Greece. His famous son, Alexander the Great, succeeded him as king at the age of 20, and travelled far and wide during his 13-year reign. By the time of his death, at the age of only 33, in 323 BC, the Macedonian empire included Persia (the country

now called Iran); Egypt, and parts of what are now India
and Afghanistan. It spread 'Hellenistic' (Greek-based)
culture to these countries and others.

   After Alexander died the Macedonian empire quickly
crumbled into smaller kingdoms, though Hellenistic culture
went on developing (did
you know that
Queen

> ## You can see Roman Greece:
>
> ☞ at the Arch of Galerius in Thessaloníki, which is covered in carvings of Roman battle scenes, and was built to honour Galerius, a deputy emperor who defeated the Persians in AD 297.
>
> ☞ at ancient Corinth in the Peloponnese. After razing the old Greek town to the ground in 46 BC, Julius Caesar built a huge new city on the site in 44 BC. It was a thriving city, with temples and theatres, until two earthquakes, in AD 375 and 521, reduced it to a pile of rubble.

Cleopatra of Egypt spoke ancient Greek, not ancient Egyptian?). In the second century BC, Greece fell to the Romans and became part of the Roman empire. The Romans admired Greek culture and learning, and so they allowed the old city states a lot of freedom to govern themselves. Greek remained the official language, rather than Latin, the language spoken throughout the Roman empire, and Greece was a fairly peaceful place for the next three centuries. Athens was still the biggest city in Greece, but new towns such as Salonika (now called Thessaloníki) were also growing in size and becoming more important.

In AD 330 the Roman empire, now converted to Christianity, was split into two: a Latin-speaking western half, centred on Rome, and a Greek-speaking eastern half, with its capital at Byzantium (renamed Constantinople, in honour of Constantine, the first Christian Roman emperor; now Istanbul in Turkey). The last Roman emperor of the western empire was deposed by the Goths in 476, but the eastern half (including Greece) became the Byzantine Empire. This empire was to become the most important power in the Mediterranean for the next 700 years, although Greece itself became a bit of a backwater.

From the 11th century onwards lots of different foreign peoples invaded Greece. It became part of the Ottoman (Turkish) empire, after Constantinople fell to the Muslim ruler, Sultan Mehmet II in 1453. (It was Mehmet who renamed the city Istanbul.) Ottoman rule lasted for nearly 400 years. During this time the Greeks were regarded as inferior to Turks and other Muslims, but they were generally left to get on with their lives, and most people continued to belong to the Greek Orthodox Church.

You can see medieval Greece:

☞ in the city of Mystrá in the Peloponnese, where there are several churches with beautiful pastel-coloured frescoes inside, showing biblical scenes. Many of them were painted by visiting artists from Italy and Constantinople.

☞ on Mount Athos, near Thessaloníki, where many of the monasteries have domed Byzantine churches. Only a few men are allowed to visit Mount Athos itself, but anyone can view the monasteries from the sea by taking a boat trip.

☞ at Monemvasía, where a beautiful Byzantine church from the 13th century, with a 16-sided dome, sits on top of the huge rock, nicknamed the 'Gibraltar of Greece'. Climb to the top for some stunning views.

Independent Greece

By the early 19th century many people in Greece were fed up with Turkish rule. In 1821 Greeks rose up against their Ottoman rulers, helped by fighters from elsewhere in Europe, who were called 'Philhellenes' ('lovers of Greece'). The most famous of these Philhellenes was the British poet

Lord Byron, who died while training Greek soldiers. After a bloody war, in which many thousands of Greeks were killed, Greece finally won its independence from the Ottoman empire in 1830. However, the newly independent country of Greece was much smaller than it is today, as big chunks of the country remained under Ottoman control until the late 1800s. Greece finally gained the borders it has today after the Balkan Wars of 1912–13, which drove the Ottomans out of Europe for good.

You can see Ottoman Greece:

☞ in Thessaloníki, where one of the most important landmarks is the White Tower on the sea front, built by the Ottomans in 1430. Today you can climb up to the roof for lovely views of the coast.

☞ at Kavála in Macedonia, where, above the traffic, you can see an acqueduct built by the Ottomans in the 16th century.

☞ at Ioańina, in northwestern Greece, which was an important town during the Ottoman years. One local commander, Aslan Pasha, built a mosque in the town, which can still be visited today.

After the Second World War broke out in 1939, Greece decided to stay neutral, but in 1940 the Italian dictator Mussolini demanded that his army should be allowed to march through Greece. The Greek Prime Minister at that time, General Ioannis Metaxas, answered by saying *óhi* (no). The date he said 'no', 28 October 1940, is still celebrated as a national holiday in Greece. From that day Greece was at war with Nazi Germany and its allies, including Italy, and from May 1941 Greece was occupied.

After it was liberated at the end of the war in 1945, Greece was immediately plunged into a bitter civil war, which lasted for four years. When it finished, the country was in a bad state after nearly ten years of war, so during the 1950s many Greeks left their remote and often very poor villages to seek work both in Athens, and abroad. There are still large Greek communities in many other countries, especially in Australia, America and Western Europe. In 1967 a group of colonels from the Greek army overthrew the government in a surprise coup d'état. This was the start of a military dictatorship, which was extremely unpopular with the Greek people. In 1974, following a student revolution and lots of demonstrations, the colonels were deposed. The Greek people then voted to have a president, instead of a king, rather like they do in France.

Despite 5,000 years of turbulent history, Greece has become a prosperous modern democracy. It is still a traditional country in many ways, especially in rural areas, but fewer people are working on the land and more in commercial companies in the cities. Girls who used to be brought up purely to be wives and mothers are now

---

You can see 19th century Greece:

☞ at Messolóngi in central Greece, the place where the English poet Lord Byron died in 1824. His heart is buried beneath his statue in the Garden of Heroes.

☞ at the Voulí, the Greek parliament building in Athens, which was built in the 1830s in classical Greek style for Greece's first modern king, Otto.

☞ on the island of Sýros, in the Cyclades, which has lots of grand neo-classical buildings, including the Town Hall and the Apollo Theatre. Sýros was a wealthy and powerful port in the 19th century, and lots of rich shipbuilders made their homes here.

> ## You can see 21st century Greece:
>
> ☞ at the amazing new Río-Antírio Bridge, which spans the Gulf of Pátras from the Greek mainland to the Peloponnese. Shortly after it was opened the bridge was crossed by the Olympic torch on its way to the opening ceremony of the 2004 Games in Athens.
>
> ☞ at the new Olympic Stadium in Athens, which was built when Athens was bidding to host the 1996 Games (they were held in Atlanta instead), but then got a new look for 2004, including a striking new roof designed by a Spanish architect called Santiago Calatrava.

encouraged to go to university and have careers.

And children and young people in Greece are starting to lead lives that are very different from those of their parents.

Local Customs: How the Greeks Live

The family

Families are very important in
Greece. Even though times are
changing, with men and
women no longer always
sticking to their
traditional roles of
breadwinner and
housewife, the
family still gives
a lot of stability to
Greek society. The idea is
that everyone takes responsibility
for one another and depends on
each other for emotional support.

It's still quite common for large
families to live together, with several generations under one
roof. Grandparents often live with their children and
grandchildren, with Granny (*Yiayia*) taking her turn with the
child care. Many young people continue to live with their
parents until they are in their 20s or 30s, because many of
them are now choosing to marry later than was the custom
in the past.

One thing is certain, wherever you go in Greece, babies
and children are always adored. So expect to be made a
fuss of.

The Greek Orthodox Church

Almost all Greeks belong to the Orthodox or Eastern Church, and Greece is the world's only officially Orthodox country. The head of the church is the Archbishop of Athens. Most people usually marry in church and have their children baptised there, as well as attending services at important times of year, such as Easter. The Orthodox Church has always been an important part of Greek life throughout history, even when Greece was being torn apart by war and foreign invasion. People feel a great deal of loyalty towards it, even if they aren't very religious.

Greece is probably the only country where more churches are being built all the time. If you can find one that is open, it is well worth having a look inside. You'll see the *iconostasis*, or altar screen, decorated with paintings of Christ and the saints. These paintings are called *icons*. Only ordained priests are allowed behind the *iconostasis*. Many churches in remote areas have only one service a year, on the name day of the patron saint of the village, when there is a feast day and dancing as well.

Unlike in the Roman Catholic Church, priests in the Orthodox Church can marry and have families. They are very respected members of their communities, and are easy to recognise by their long black robes, long beards and tall black hats. Priests often have second jobs in addition to their religious duties.

During a Greek Orthodox wedding the bride and groom stand before the priest. White crowns bound together by a white ribbon are placed on their heads and the *koumbáros*, or best man, exchanges them back and forth. The newlyweds are then led around the altar three times, while the guests throw rice and flower petals over them. After congratulating the bride and groom, the guests are given a small gift, a *bonboniéra*, a little bundle of candied almonds. The church service is followed by... yes, you guessed it... feasting and dancing.

Baptisms are also cause for great celebration. The baby might not be quite so happy about things, because the priest dunks the baby completely in holy water three times. Children are almost always given the name of a grandparent. For extra protection from the forces of evil, babies often wear a *filaktó* or amulet, in the form of a blue glass bead that looks like an eye.

Music and kéfi

You don't have to spend much time in Greece to realise how important music is to Greeks, young and old. It's hard to explain exactly what *kéfi* means, though. The word describes the way in which Greeks have a tendency to break into song and dance at the least excuse.

Folk music is very popular and every region has its own type of dance and music, and its own traditional songs, which are usually about love, marriage, death and heroes. These are performed at weddings, at baptisms and at the local saint's day celebrations called *panegýri*. Many folk dances go back to ancient times too, and can have quite complicated steps. You might find yourself being asked to join in, so be prepared!

Musicians at festivals might play a stringed instrument called a *bouzoúki*, which sounds typically Greek: it makes the sound that you probably conjure up when you think of Greek music. There's also a small harp called a *sandoúri*, which is played with hammers, and a Greek version of the bagpipes, called a *tsamboúna*.

But Greeks don't need the excuse of a wedding or festival to break into song and dance. They will do so any time, any place, anywhere. It's *kéfi*, you see.

The períptero

The *períptero* is a kind of kiosk you'll spot in every Greek town and village, where people gather to chat, to make phone calls or even just to grab a few minutes in the shade. You can also buy anything from a bottle of water or beer to ice-cream, snacks, aspirin, mosquito killers, magazines and newspapers, maps, guides, postcards and stamps, shoelaces, batteries, sunglasses, soap, toothpaste and rolls of film. If you run out of anything when you're out and about in Greece, head for the *períptero*. Chances are that it will be open, and you will be in luck!

Icons

No statues are allowed in Orthodox churches, but, if you go inside one, you'll notice straight away that there are lots of holy pictures of Christ, the Virgin Mary and the saints. These pictures are called *icons* (*icon* means 'image'), and many are old and valuable. They often also have little

gold and silver plaques called *táma* attached to them. These are the gifts of those who have had, or hope to have, their prayers answered. You'll also see *icons* in Greek homes, sometimes with a little oil lamp or candle burning below them; and also in offices, shops and even in buses and taxis. Many fishing boats carry an *icon* of *Ayíos Nikólaos* (St Nicholas), because he is the patron saint and protector of sailors. Some *icons* are reputed to be responsible for miracles, including a famous *icon* of the Virgin Mary on the island of Tínos.

Plane trees

There is usually at least one plane tree in the centre of every Greek village. It's the place where people get together to talk, exchange gossip and chew over the issues of the day. As many plane trees are hundreds of years old, they've probably heard some things in their time. There is even a Greek expression, *Cheréte mou ton plátano,* or 'Send my regards to the plane tree.' This loosely translates as 'You're having a laugh' or 'You're kidding me', probably because the old tree has heard all this nonsense before.

The plane, a beautiful tall tree with spreading branches, is loved by the Greeks as a source of life for it grows only in places where there is plenty of fresh water, sun and warmth. In the heat of the Greek midday sun, it's also very pleasant to sit with a drink under the shade of its spreading branches.

Clothes

Most Greeks wear exactly the same sort of clothes as you do. You'll notice, though, that some older Greeks wear black when they go out, and the women are often draped in black shawls. This is to show respect for members of their families who have died.

The Greek national dress is a white shirt, a red hat and a white skirt called a *fustanella,* and that's for the men. They also wear pompoms on their shoes. This costume is worn for special celebrations and dances. It was worn by the Greeks who fought for their freedom in the Greek War of Independence, so it is treated with great respect.

The 'evil eye'

Many Greeks are very superstitious, and one of the things that they are most wary of is the 'evil eye'. You'll probably see blue glass amulets in the form of eyes hanging around – from the rear-view mirrors in cars, painted onto boats, round the necks of children and babies, and even on horses and donkeys. These are designed to ward off the influence of the evil eye, which, it is believed, brings bad luck and worse.

Be careful when paying compliments in Greece. For similar reasons, it is considered bad luck to say how pretty, handsome, elegant or well someone looks – especially a baby or a child – because this might attract the jealous attention of the gods. When admiring something, Greeks make a pretend spitting sound (sort of 'phtoo, phtoo, phtoo') to distract this envy.

Olives with everything

The history and culture of Greece is completely entwined with olives and olive trees. They pop up everywhere. The goddess Athena beat off the rival god Poseidon in a fight to decide which one of them the newly built city of Athens should be named after. The citizens decided that Athena's gift of an olive tree would be more use to them than Poseidon's pressie of a salt-water spring – what use is that? The tree that Athena planted on the Acropolis would provide fruit, oil and wood: an olive tree has grown on the same spot ever since.

In ancient Greece, the olive tree was considered sacred, and anyone found guilty of uprooting or destroying one was sentenced to death. For more than 5,000 years the olive tree has been the most used and most loved tree in Greece. It also symbolises wisdom, triumph and peace (think of Noah's Ark and the dove carrying an olive branch for peace after the Flood).

One of the reasons why the olive tree has been so prized by the Greeks is that every part of the tree can be used for something. Olive oil can be used for cooking, as fuel for oil lamps, and for medicine. The olives can be eaten and the leaves can be used for making tea. The wood can be used for fires.

By tradition, an olive tree is planted to mark the birth of a baby. By the time the child starts school, at the age of six, the tree is ready to produce fruit. Unlike people, olive trees can live for hundreds of years.

Olive trees need very warm average temperatures to survive, so they grow very happily throughout Greece, where there are about 137 million of them! The olives are harvested every year, between November and March, and Greece is the only country in Europe that allows government employees time off to return to their villages for the olive harvest.

Some of the olives are used to make olive oil, one of Greece's major exports in ancient times and today. Greece is the world's largest exporter of extra virgin olive oil. Plenty of the stuff stays in Greece too: the Greeks get through more olive oil than any other country in the world.

Some olives are harvested early before they are ripe: these are the green ones. The others are picked when they are ripe and black in colour. Make sure you try them when you are in Greece. They are a bit of an acquired taste: if you don't like them at first, try them again later, because you might suddenly get a taste for them. Then you, too, can have olives with everything, just like the Greeks.

Sign language

Learning to speak Greek is difficult enough, with all those unfamilar letters and sounds to get your head (and tongue) around. What makes things even more complicated is that Greeks speak a whole other language with their hands and faces. For example, when Greeks want to say no they often click their tongues, raise their eyebrows and tip their heads backwards. For yes they might do a forward nod with their head tilted to one side. If someone doesn't hear or understand you properly, they might shake their heads from side to side and say *Oríste*? ('Pardon?'). Just generally when talking, Greeks make lots of gestures: on the whole, they are not quiet, reserved people!

Wayside shrines

If you're driving through Greece, you'll probably see little shrines by the side of the road. These are called *ikonostáses*, and they might contain a saint's icon, an oil lamp and a box of matches. Often they were put there by someone who wanted to thank a saint for an answered prayer. They might also show that there is a church nearby.

Sponges

A great thing to buy in Greece is one of those natural sponges to use in the bath. They are lovely and soft, fun to play with, and much cheaper than those you get at home. But where do they come from?

Sponges are sea creatures and fishing for them is a dangerous business, which has been going on in Greece since ancient times. Back then, sponge-divers strapped heavy stones to their chests to weigh them down to the sea bed, where they speared the sponges with tridents and then gave the signal that they wanted to be pulled back to the surface. Many sponge-divers drowned in the process.

The last fleet of sponge-divers left in Greece today is on the Dodecanese island of Kálymnos. It is hard to make a living from sponge-diving nowadays, because most people use artificial sponges, which are much cheaper. Now only a few boats leave from Kálymnos each spring for a four-month voyage around the Aegean in search of sponges.

When sponges are pulled out of the sea they are smelly and black. They are then squeezed until their skeletons (the part you use in the bath) are clean. The yellow colour comes from bleaching them: if you want a really strong sponge, buy a natural brown one. Look for the densest texture and the smallest holes. Some shops even have buckets of water on hand, so that you can test them out.

The MONSTER in the MAZE

An old Greek story tells of a strange creature called the Minotaur. Half bull, half man, and all mean, he lived imprisoned in...

The Labyrinth - a maze of caves, a cave of mazes, deep beneath the Palace of Knossos on the island of Crete

HΩME SWEET HΩME

The Minotaur's mum was Pasiphaë, queen of Crete

He was related to Poseidon, god of the sea

Did they ever pop round for tea and biscuits? Did they heck

Every now and then, to keep the king of Crete happy, the city of Athens had to send a few of its young citizens to the Labyrinth

They'd get lost, of course, and soon they'd get dead

Eventually the Minotaur was slain by the flashy Athenian hero Theseus, and that was that

DODGY HAIRDO!

JEALOUS!

A happy ending for everyone

Well, almost everyone

Well, even a monster has to eat, right? Yes, dinner was a rare and messy affair

The Minotaur had been part human, part animal, part god. Different from anyone or anything else. A freak. He had to be sorted out, of course - he was out of order. So it was just as well. But in a way it was a shame, too

There was a bit less wonder in the world once there was no more monster in the maze

A School Day in Greece

Greek children have to go to school from the age of six until they are 15. They attend primary school (*dimótiko scholéio*) until the age of 12, when they start at lower secondary school (*gymnásio* – nothing to do with keeping fit!). It's possible to leave school at 15, but, if you want to carry on studying for more qualifications, you can either go to a technical school (TEE or *technica epaggelmatics ekpaideftiría* – let's stick to TEE, shall we?), or a high school, called a *lykeío*. The word *lykeío* comes from the ancient Greek name for the temple of Apollo in Athens, next to which Aristotle started his famous school, known in English as the Lyceum.

A typical school day in Greece starts at 8.15 or 8.30 am and finishes at 1.30 pm – yes, 1.30 pm! Before you turn green with envy, bear in mind that Greek children get more homework than you do, to make up for the shorter school day. What's more, a lot of Greek parents are so keen for their children to do well at school and get good jobs later on that they send them to private lessons in the afternoons and evenings, to do some extra studying. Yuk! Greek children do get good long holidays however: 2 weeks at Easter, 2 weeks at Christmas, and a whole 10 weeks over the summer!

In some rural places there isn't enough classroom space for all the local children to go to school at the same time, so some have to go in the morning, the rest in the afternoon. Before 1981 children had to wear a uniform in the Greek national colours of blue and white. Nowadays they can wear what they like, within reason.

At the beginning of the school year many pupils receive a special blessing from the local priest, who dips a sprig of basil in holy water and then touches the children with it. Wonder if it helps with all that homework too?

Fabulous Buildings and Sights

The ancient Greeks built no less than five of the Seven Wonders of the Ancient World: the Colossus of Rhodes; the statue of Zeus at Olympus; the Mausoleum at Halicarnassus and the temple of Artemis at Ephesus (both in what is now Turkey); and the Pharos lighthouse at Alexandria (in Egypt). Unfortunately, not one of these ancient wonders is still standing today, but there's still masses to see.

Athens

Athens became the capital of modern Greece in 1834, after the Greeks won their independence from Turkey. Though it was an important city in ancient times, Athens had fallen into ruin during the many centuries when Greece was ruled by the Ottomans and other foreign powers. After 1834 the population grew very quickly, and today Athens is one of Europe's largest cities, with a population of more than three million. Over one third of Greeks live in or near Athens, and in the summer thousands of tourists come to visit its monuments and museums.

It's a fantastic time to visit Athens, because the city underwent a massive spring-cleaning and modernisation programme for the 2004 Olympics There are hundreds of things to see in Athens, many of them thousands of years old. If you only have a short time in the city, make sure that you don't miss:

The Acropolis

The ancient city grew up around the huge limestone cliff, 156 metres high, which stands in the centre of Athens. It was home to the Acropolis, or 'High City', and it was here that the ancient Greeks built beautiful temples in honour of the goddess Athena. They believed that Athena protected the city, and of course, it is from Athena that Athens gets its name.

The most important temple on the Acropolis was the Parthenon. It is still one of the most famous and recognisable buildings in the world, and is probably the first one that comes to mind when you think about Greece. The Parthenon was completed in 438 BC and has stood above the city ever since. Its name means 'of the virgin', because it had a special room at the back for the virgin priestesses who looked after it.

The man responsible for building the Parthenon and many of the other buildings on the Acropolis was Pericles. For almost 30 years in the 5th century BC, Pericles was the First Magistrate of Athens. In 458 BC he asked one of the most famous sculptors of the day, Phidias, to create the Parthenon, with the help of two of the finest architects in Athens, Ictinus and Callicrates. Phidias also sculpted a huge

gold and ivory statue of Athena to stand inside the
Parthenon. The statue was more than 12 metres high, and
showed the goddess standing upright with a spear in her left
hand and a shield in her right. (It was destroyed long ago.)

To the ancient Greeks a beautiful building was one which
was symmetrical and in proportion, so they built according
to strict mathematical ratios. Unbelievably, there are no
straight lines in the whole building, because, said the ancient
Greeks, there are none in nature. If you look carefully, you'll
see that lines that might look straight at first are actually
slightly curved.

The Parthenon was constructed of white marble and put
together without the cement
we use today. The
round stone
drums

that make up the huge columns have a hole in each end big enough to take a short round stick that connects two drums together. During the building the blocks were turned round and round against each other until they ground to a perfect fit. Clever stuff.

In ancient times Greek temples such as the Parthenon would have looked very different from the grey-white ruins you see today. They were painted in bright reds, blues, greens and yellows, and shimmered with gold. Today, after being covered with scaffolding for years, the Parthenon can be seen in all its glory, after the Greeks made huge efforts to get repairs done in order to have it uncovered in time for the 2004 Olympics.

Facing the Parthenon is the Erechtheion, another very important and beautiful temple. It was built on the most sacred site on the whole Acropolis, the place where Athena was said to have planted an olive tree when fighting the god Poseidon for possession of the city. Around the south porch are the famous Caryatids, gorgeous statues of women generally thought to be some of the finest examples of Greek art. The six that you can see are copies, but four of the originals are in the Acropolis Museum.

The Acropolis is also home to the Temple of Athena Nike. (Yes, the trainer people pinched the name from the Greek word meaning 'victory'.) The temple was built in 426–421 BC to commemorate Athens's victory over the Persians.

If you're a fan of the stage, make tracks to the Theatre of Dionysus, which is cut into the cliff face below the main Acropolis. This was the birthplace of ancient Greek tragedy and comedy: Aeschylus, Sophocles, Euripides

and Aristophanes all had their plays performed here during the annual Dionysia festival. The remains you see today are of an enormous theatre built on the site by the Romans, in which 17,000 people could watch gladiators fight to the death.

Apart from all the ancient buildings to see, it is also worth climbing the Acropolis just for the wonderful views from the top over Athens and the surrounding area.

Sýntagma Square

On one side of 'Constitution Square', known as *Platéia Syntágmatos* in Greek, you'll see the Voulí building, home to the Greek Parliament and the Tomb of the Unknown Soldier, which was unveiled on Independence Day (25 March) in 1932. It is guarded by *evzones* or National Guards, who are always on patrol in their famous skirted uniforms and red shoes with pompoms. It is *not* OK to make fun of their clothes, or the strange way they stride up and down. You wouldn't laugh if you had to parade up and down in the hot sun all day!

The *Platéia Syntágmatos* is the hub of modern Athens, and the place where all the bus, tram and metro routes come together. It was also the focus for the huge national street party that kicked off when the Greek football team won the 2004 European Championships. Hooray!

Not far away is the Presidential Palace, which was the home of the Greek royal family until King Constantine II gave up the throne in 1967. It is now the official residence of the President of Greece, currently a man called Constantinos Stephanopoulos.

Kallimármaro Stadium

Built in a big horseshoe shape, the Kallimármaro Stadium dates from AD 140. It was restored and used for the first modern Olympic Games, which took place in Athens in 1896. For the 2004 Athens Olympics it was used for the exciting last lap of the marathon.

Attica and central Greece

Attica is the region around Athens. Its coast is very popular with Athenians at weekends and during the holidays, when they head out of the city in their thousands to escape the heat and pollution. Further inland and to the north are some of Greece's most important sites, including the ancient oracle at Delphi, as well as some beautiful areas rarely explored by tourists, such as Epirus, and Zagóri in the Píndus Mountains.

Cape Soúnion

Cape Soúnion is at the very southernmost point of the Attica region. According to legend, it was the place from which Aegeus, King of Athens, watched and waited for the return of his son Theseus, who had gone off to Crete to fight the Minotaur, a monster that was half-man, half-bull. Before he left, Theseus had agreed to hoist a white sail to signal that he was returning victorious. Unfortunately he forgot, and when Aegeus saw his son's ship sailing towards him with a black sail, he thought that Theseus was dead, and threw himself off the high rocky cape into the sea below. At least he got to have the sea named after him: the Aegean, no less.

Soúnion is also the site of a temple dedicated to the sea god Poseidon. Lord Byron carved his name on one of the pillars in 1810.

Delphi

According to legend, when Zeus released two eagles from opposite ends of the world their flight paths crossed in the sky above Delphi. From then on Delphi was believed to be the centre of the Earth, and it was also the home of the god Apollo. From the end of the 8th century BC, people from all over the ancient world came to Delphi to consult Apollo about the important decisions and problems in their lives: a sort of ancient fortune-telling. The famous Delphic oracle was the means through which, it was believed, worshippers in the temple or sanctuary of Apollo could hear the words of the god. The words were actually spoken by the priestesses or Pythia of

Delphi, all of whom were aged over 50 and went into trances as they sat above the volcanic fumes coming out of the ground here. Visitors would pay some money and sacrifice an animal on the altar in the temple, before getting to ask their all-important questions. The oracle continued to be important to the ancient Greeks until Roman times, and was only finally abolished when Greece became a Christian country, in the 4th century AD. Today Delphi is still a beautiful place, where you can visit the ruins of the Temple of Apollo and walk along the Sacred Way that leads to it. There's also the remains of a stadium, the site of the Pythian Games, which were the second biggest in ancient Greece after the Olympics.

All this talk of 'Pythia' and 'Pythian' is probably making you think of pythons. And you'd be right to! The first name for the oracle at Delphi was Pytho, because, so the story goes, it was guarded by a hero-snake called Pytho. Apollo decided to get rid of Pytho and take over the oracle himself, so he disguised himself as a dolphin (*delphinos* in ancient Greek – now you know where Delphi got its name) in order to get there from the island of Delos and shoot Pytho with his arrows.

Metéora

Metéora, which means 'rocks in the air', is one of the most spectacular sights in the whole of Greece, and has been used as a location in several films, including the James Bond film *For Your Eyes Only*. Huge natural sandstone rocks rise out of the plain, which, from the 10th century AD onwards, were used as a get-away-from-it-all religious retreat. The first inhabitant was a hermit called Barnabas, who lived in a cave in one of the rocks. Then, in 1382, a monk called Athanásios founded and built a monastery on one of the high pinnacles of rock: legend has it that he got up there on the back of an eagle. Twenty-three more monasteries followed. For

centuries the only way to get goods and people in and out was by a winch system and a net bag. Nowadays you can climb to the monasteries by steep paths and stairs.

The Peloponnese

This is a large, mountainous region almost separated from the rest of mainland Greece by a very long sea inlet, made up of the Gulf of Patras and the Gulf of Corinth. Is it an island or isn't it? Officially it's a peninsula, joined to the rest of Greece by a narrow neck of land (an isthmus). However, it is actually cut in two by the Corinth Canal so really it's an island. Built in 1893, the Corinth Canal allows some ships to pass from the Aegean to the Ionian sea and the western Mediterranean. However it isn't wide enough for oil tankers or large cruise liners, so they still have to go the long way round!

The Río–Antírio Bridge

A spectacular new bridge now links mainland Greece with the Peloponnese, between the towns of Antírio and Río. The bridge is 2,252 metres long and has four columns supported by cables along its length. Its architects had several problems to solve when designing the bridge, including how to make sure it wouldn't collapse if there was an earthquake. Finally they came up with a revolutionary solution. The piers that support the bridge rest on a bed of gravel, instead of being buried in the seabed, so they can absorb any movement.

The bridge was finished just in time for the Olympic flame to cross it on its way to Athens for the 2004 Games. One of the proud torchbearers across the bridge was Otto Rehhagel, the German coach of the Greek national football team that won Euro 2004.

Ancient Olympia

If you're a fan of athletics, you must make a pilgrimage to Olympia. Named after the home of the gods, Mount Olympus (which, confusingly, is in another part of Greece altogether), it was the place where the ancient Olympic Games took place. Being ancient Greece, it was also home to lots of temples. The first Games took place in 776 BC. The stadium you can see the site of today was built in the 5th century BC and could hold 45,000 spectators. There were no seats; everyone just sat on the ground,

except for the umpires, who sat on a raised platform. You can see the original marks for the starting and finishing lines, and even the indentations made for the runners' toes. As well as running races, chariot and horse races were also held. You can also see the remains of the Palaestra, where wrestlers, boxers and longjumpers trained, and the Gymnasium, where athletes trained for the discus, javelin and the running races. The walls were inscribed with the names of those who had won past events, to spur them on to great things. The Olympic flame for the modern Olympic Games is still lit here, and then carried to the city hosting the next Games, sometimes on the other side of the world!

Mycenae

Mycenae was an important regional power between 1500 and 1200 BC. It became wealthy through seafaring and trading. Its famous fortified palace complex, with its massive walls, lay buried for around 3,000 years until it was uncovered by the German archaeologist Heinrich Schliemann in 1874. Legend has it that Mycenae was founded by the hero Perseus, who was out for a walk one day when a mushroom (or *mykos* in Greek) popped out of the ground, followed by a spring. Perseus decided to build a new city there and name it after the mushroom. At Mycenae today you can see the famous Lion Gate, and also lots of tombs where the rich and powerful were buried with a whole pile of weapons and masses of gold. Mycenae seems to have been a fabulously wealthy place – Homer himself tells us it was 'rich in gold'. Many of the treasures dug up by Schliemann can be seen in the National Museum in Athens, including the famous death mask of Agamemnon.

Epidauros

If you were feeling unwell or stressed out in ancient Greece and you could afford it, you might have treated yourself to a few days at Epidauros. From around the 6th century BC the Sanctuary of Epidauros was a big healing and religious centre dedicated to the god of healing, Asklepios, a sort of ancient Greek health spa. The main reason to visit Epidauros today is to see its superb ancient theatre, which has a perfectly preserved circular *orchestra* or stage, and 55 rows of seats steeply built one on top of the other in a semi-circle. Its shape means that the acoustics are fantastic: if you visit Epidauros you must try them out. Send someone to sit at the very top of the theatre (it helps if they are fit!). Then stand on the stage and speak in a normal voice. If there aren't too many people doing the same thing, they should be able to hear you perfectly, even though you are far below them! The theatre is still used today: every July and August Epidauros plays host to a festival of ancient drama, including performances of plays by Sophocles, Aeschylus, Euripedes and Aristophanes.

Monemvasía

A fortified town built on two levels on a massive rock that rises 350 metres above the sea, it is close to the end of one of the fingers of the Peloponnese peninsula. The rock of Monemvasía was severed from the mainland by an earthquake in AD 375 and stayed cut off until a causeway was built in the 6th century. The town had its heyday during the 15th century, when it was home to 50,000 people, many of whom made a very

comfortable living, thank you very much, from being pirates. Today you can walk the old city walls and climb the zig-zagging path that takes you up to the rock's summit, where a beautiful 13th-century church is all that is left standing in the upper town.

Northern Greece

Thessaloníki

Thessaloníki, which used to be called Salonica, is Greece's second-biggest city and also a busy port. It is the capital of the Macedonia region, and was ruled by the Ottomans from 1430 until 1912. It has lots of beautiful churches – one of them is the largest church in the whole of Greece – and a brilliant Archaeological Museum. Here you'll find lots about Alexander the Great, some beautiful gold objects and some gorgeous mosaics.

Mount Athos

Three fingers of land point into the sea to the south of Thessaloníki, in an area called Chalkidikí. The finger on the right is Mount Athos, a beautiful but very strange place, which the Greeks call 'Holy Mountain'. It is actually a separate republic from the rest of Greece, ruled by the 1,700 monks who live in the 20 monasteries around its shores. Only adult males can visit Mount Athos, and then only with permission (even female animals – apart from hens and cats – are not allowed!). You can however, take a boat trip around the peninsula to see some of its impressive monasteries from a distance. Many of them look more like castles.

The Greek islands

The islands are among the most visited parts of Greece.

'Island-hopping' holidays are very popular: basically you hop on and off the regular ferries between the islands, and just go where you please!

Crete

Crete is the largest island in Greece and also the most southerly island in the Aegean Sea. It is less than 300km from the coast of North Africa, so it is one of the hottest places in Greece. It's a long and narrow island with some high mountains along the middle. The Cretan people are very proud of their island, which was not officially part of Greece until 1913, and so has its own culture, music and dances, and even its own dialect of Greek.

In ancient times Crete was a happening place: Zeus, the greatest of the gods, was born here, so they say, and the Minoan civilisation – the first proper European civilisation – was founded on the island.

The great palace at Knossos was the capital of the mysterious Minoan civilisation, which was named after the legendary King Minos. An English archaeologist called Sir Arthur Evans spent 30 years uncovering the remains of Knossos, which you can visit today near the city of Irákleio. There's a throne room, a theatre, some gorgeous frescoes, baths and a drainage system. Amazingly, it's thought that Knossos even had flushing toilets.

According to legend, Knossos also had an underground

labyrinth of tunnels inhabited by a scary creature called the Minotaur, who was half-man, half-bull, and required a diet of young men from Athens, who were sacrificed to him. The hero Theseus eventually put a stop to this by killing the Minotaur with the help of a Cretan princess called Ariadne.

The spectacular Samariá Gorge is the longest ravine in Europe. It's open from May to October, and closed at other times of year because of the danger of flooding. If you're fit, you can hike its 18-km length in one day, as long as you take plenty of water with you and wear good shoes: it's a tough walk. Along the way there are tiny chapels and rare wild flowers, and, if you're very, very lucky, you might see a *kri-kri*, or Cretan wild goat.

The Cyclades

Those postcard pictures you see everywhere, with whitewashed sugar-cube houses and blue-domed churches against a deep blue sky, were probably taken on one of the Cyclades islands. The name 'Cyclades' comes from the Greek word *kyklos*, meaning circle, because the islands are arranged in a ring. Most of them have wonderful sandy beaches and so attract many visitors in the summer. Three of the most popular are Myknonos, Páros and Sifnos, but Delos and Santoríni are interesting too.

Delos is a tiny uninhabited island in the middle of the Cyclades. It is one of the most important places in the whole of Greece. According to legend, the twin gods Artemis and Apollo were

64

born here. A famous festival called the Delia took place on the island, during which games and music were played in honour of Apollo. You can take a boat trip from Mykonos to visit the ruins today: there's a temple, five famous Lion statues (there used to be nine, but one is in Venice and the rest went missing) and a theatre.

Between 1500 and 1450 BC one of the biggest volcanic eruptions ever took place on the island of Santoríni (or Thíra, as it was called then). A massive explosion blew the middle out of the island and left a huge crater called a caldera. The explosion caused earthquakes across the Aegean, and a devastating tsunami that destroyed the Minoan civilisation on Crete, not far to the south. Santoríni today is a stunning island with white villages clinging to its steep volcanic cliffs. At sunset they have fantastic views of the caldera below: you could call Santoríni the island that launched a thousand postcards!

The Dodecanese

There are 12 main islands in the Dodecanese. Which is good, because *dhódheka* actually means '12'! Most of them are closer to Turkey than they are to the Greek mainland. In fact, for much of their history the Dodecanese weren't part of Greece at all, and they only joined up with the rest of the country in 1948. Before that, Italy occupied the islands for 35 years from 1912 onwards.

The most popular islands with tourists are Rhodes and Kos (where Kos lettuce comes from). Rhodes is the largest Dodecanese island and attracts lots of tourists because of its sandy beaches. There's lots of history here, too. Between 1306 and 1522 the Crusader Knights of St John were in charge here, and they built a medieval walled city (now part of the capital, Rhodes Town) and lots of castles. The Ottomans defeated the Knights of St John after a great siege in 1522, and they added some mosques and a *hammam* or

Turkish bath to Rhodes Town.

Rhodes was also the site of one of the Wonders of the Ancient World: the Colossus of Rhodes. The Colossus was a huge statue of Helios, the god who was said to drive the chariot of the Sun. It was about 40m tall and, though we don't know for sure what it actually looked like, most drawings show it standing with one foot on either side of the harbour, with ships sailing through its legs. An earthquake in 227 BC caused it to topple over, and that was the end of that.

Pátmos has been nicknamed the 'Jerusalem of the Aegean', and is a very holy island. The reason is that St John the Apostle is said to have arrived here in AD 95 and lived in a cave for a while. There he wrote the Book of Revelation, the final book of the New Testament, which is all about how the world is supposed to end. According to the legend, St John saw a vision of fire and brimstone in the cave, and heard the voice of God coming from a cleft in the rock.

Nísyros is worth a trip to see the huge crater of its volcano, left after a violent eruption in 1422. According to mythology, Nísyros was formed when the god Poseidon picked up a piece of Kos in a temper and dropped it on the giant Polyvotis, whom he was fighting with at the time. Polyvotis is said to be living under the island to this day, sighing and fuming. If you walk across the crater of the volcano, you'll certainly see steam and hot springs. The beaches of Nísyros are made of black volcanic sand and dark pebbles. There are also a lot of pumice stones lying around, which you can take home as a souvenir to use in the bath!

The Ionian islands

The Ionian islands are the ones on the western side of the Greek mainland, and they are also the greenest of the Greek islands, with lots of olive groves and cypress trees. They have a long history of being visited by tourists: even the Romans used to holiday on the Ionian islands. The islands have a slightly different history from the rest of Greece. They were never ruled over by the Ottomans, but instead the Venetians were in charge for more than 400 years until 1797, when the French and then the British took over. In 1864 the islands finally became part of Greece. Today these different influences can still be seen. On Corfu, for example, you can admire Venetian buildings, drink coffee in French cafés and even play cricket. There aren't many archaeological sites on the islands, so tourists come mainly for beach holidays.

Corfu is the largest Ionian island and the most popular with foreign tourists, who come in their planeloads to enjoy its lovely scenery and wonderful sandy beaches. If you stay on the island for a while, you're bound to come across at least one person called Spíros. This is because lots of babies are named after the island's patron saint, St Spyrídon, whose mummified body rests in a church in Corfu Town.

Zákynthos is famous for its rare green loggerhead turtles, which migrate from North Africa to nest and lay their eggs in the soft sand of the island's beaches. Unfortunately, because there are now so many tourists on the island the turtles can no longer go about their business undisturbed, so they are becoming a threatened species. Conservationists are trying to make sure that tourists don't use certain parts of the beaches to give the turtles a chance to lay their eggs – and so have lots of baby turtles – in peace.

Great Greeks, Ancient and Modern

Ancient Greeks

Achilles

Achilles was a warrior and the greatest Greek hero of the
Trojan War. Mind you, he had a bit of an advantage.
According to legend, he couldn't be wounded on any part of
his body except for one tender spot at the back of his heel.
The story goes that, after killing lots of Trojans, including
their most famous fighter, Hector, Achilles was finally killed
by a poison arrow to the heel. To this day the big tendon that
runs from the heel to the calf muscle (the one that footballers
are always injuring) is called the 'Achilles tendon'.

Homer

Nothing to do with *The Simpsons*! Homer, who probably
lived in the 700s BC, created the two most famous poems in
the whole of Greek literature: *The Iliad* and *The Odyssey*. *The
Iliad* tells the story of the Trojan War and how the Greek hero
Achilles met his death. It was as important to the ancient
Greeks as the Bible and Shakespeare are to us today. They

learned to recite it at school and wrote plays based on it. *The Odyssey* tells of the adventures of the Greek hero Odysseus on his way home from the Trojan War. Homer, who is reputed to have been blind, probably based his poems on stories about the war that were passed down by word of mouth from one generation to the next.

There are still arguments about where Homer lived, how he created the poems and when they were first written down, but there aren't many arguments about the wonderful stories they contain.

Sappho

Sappho was born on the island of Lesbos around 630 BC, and was one of the greatest of all Greek poets. When she was young she got involved in politics, and in 600 BC she was banished to Sicily for being too outspoken. She married and had a daughter, but after her husband died she returned to Lesbos and opened a marriage school for young ladies dedicating many of her poems to her pupils.

Aesop

It is hard to be certain, but Aesop was probably an ex-slave from the island of Samos, who lived during the sixth century BC. He travelled around Greece telling stories with morals such as 'Slow and steady wins the race' ('The Hare and the Tortoise'); 'Don't count your chickens until they are hatched' ('The Milkmaid and Her Pail'); and 'Look before you leap' ('The Fox and the Goat'). The legend is that Aesop died

when he was thrown
off a cliff in Delphi,
but no one knows
who did it, or why.
Despite the fact that none
of his fables were written
down until about 200 years
after he is supposed to have
lived, they are still widely read and
the morals still hold true.

Pythagoras

Pythagoras (c. 582–497 BC) was a
brilliant Greek mathematician
from the island of Sámos.
Pythagoras believed that everything
in the universe was determined by
numbers and mathematical
relationships. He developed many
mathematical principles: you may
even have used some of his methods in geometry lessons!
Pythagoras was also a vegetarian, and believed that both
animals and people have souls that can be reborn again and
again.

Herodotus

Herodotus lived from 485 to 425 BC and came from the city
of Halikarnassos (now the Turkish city of Bodrum). He is
famous as one of the first historians: in fact he has often been
called 'the father of history' (our English word 'history'
comes from the Greek word for enquiry). Herodotus
travelled widely, and was one of the first people to write
down and record historical events accurately, and to try to
interpret them for future generations. His book *The Histories*
is still widely read today.

Hippocrates

Hippocrates, who lived from around 460 to 390 BC, was a doctor who ran a school of medicine on the island of Kos. He taught people how to care for their patients by paying attention to their 'symptoms' (the Greek word for 'signs'). His students took an oath before they were allowed to work as doctors, something along the lines of 'I will use treatment to help the sick and I will not give poison to anyone.' Until only a few years ago new doctors still had to swear a similar Hippocratic Oath.

Pericles

Pericles was a brilliant leader and public speaker who was in charge of Athens during the 5th century BC and was very popular with his people. Pericles was full of bright ideas: many of the great buildings you can see on the Acropolis in Athens today, including the Parthenon, were his idea. However, he is best remembered today as one of the founders of democracy, a system of government used in most countries today.

Socrates

Socrates, who lived between 470 and 399 BC, was an Athenian war hero and the greatest philosopher of his day. He taught his pupils, including Plato, about truth by asking them questions to make them think hard about their beliefs. Unfortunately, many people in Athens got fed up with the way his pupils were starting to question the gods and democracy. He was tried and sentenced to death for 'introducing new gods and corrupting the young'. Socrates refused to change his ways, even though he was given several more chances to clear his name. Eventually he chose to die by drinking poison made from a plant called hemlock.

Plato

Plato was an Athenian philosopher who lived from 427 to 347 BC. Plato was a nickname meaning 'broad', which he got because he was good at wrestling. Plato loved the Spartan way of doing things and founded a school in Athens called the Academy (from which we get the word 'academic'), where he taught philosophy and mathematics. His pupils included Aristotle, and, unusually for the time, several women. Plato's writings have been very influential down the ages and are often about how to make the world a better place. One of his ideas was that behind our world lies an 'ideal world' much better than the one we live in.

Alexander the Great

Alexander was the son of King Philip II of Macedonia, a region in the far north of Greece. His father invaded the Greek lands to the south and ruled over them until he was murdered by one of his officers in 336 BC. Alexander succeeded his father as king at the age of 20. He was an energetic leader and a superb fighter who had also had an excellent education from his tutor, the famous philosopher Aristotle. Alexander admired the heroes of Greek legend, such as Achilles, and was determined to follow in their footsteps. He decided to invade the huge Persian empire, which lay to the east of Greece, and within 11 years his armies had conquered Persia (now called Iran); Egypt (where he founded the city of Alexandria); and parts of modern India and Afghanistan. Among the things that Alexander brought back to Europe from his travels in Asia were bananas, cotton and sugar. Alexander the Great died at the age of 33 in the city of Babylon (in what is now Iraq) from a fever. His empire quickly crumbled after his death, but at its height it was the greatest the world had ever known. Legend has it that Alexander also invented shaving, because he thought that beards gave the enemy something to grab hold of!

Aristotle

Aristotle was a famous Greek philosopher. He left his birthplace, Athens, to become tutor to the young Alexander the Great, but then spent the rest of his life in the city, where became a teacher and founded a famous school called the Lyceum. He is famous for dividing scientific knowledge into the separate subjects we study today: for example, biology, zoology and physics. He also taught that science should be based, not on guesswork, but on observations and experiments, a principle that scientists still hold dear to this day.

Archimedes

Archimedes was a mathematician who lived in the Greek colony of Syracuse on the island of Sicily. He is most famous for jumping out of his bath and running down the streek naked, shouting *Eureka* ('I have found it'), when he realised that, for every bit of his body that went into his very full

bath, an equal amount of water spilled over the top.
Archimedes also invented some amazing war machines and
the 'Archimedes Screw', a device that lifts water from one
level to another, and that is still in use today. He was killed
by a Roman soldier when the Romans captured Syracuse in
212 BC.

Pausanias

Pausanias was a Greek writer and traveller who wrote one
of the first-ever guidebooks in the 2nd century AD. His
travels took him as far as Egypt, Italy and the Middle East.
He wrote his book, *Description of Greece*, for rich Roman
travellers who fancied seeing something of his country. He
writes so well about the places he visited, and in such detail,
that many archaeological
sites have been
discovered thanks to
his descriptions.

Santa Claus

Of course Santa Claus exists! He's a
Greek who also goes by the name of
St Nicholas, or Nikólaos,
if you want to be exact.
He was born in around
AD 300 in Asia Minor
and was one of the
youngest men ever to
become a priest. He
was very generous to
the poor and legend
has it that he even
used to throw bags of gold
down their chimneys.
Later he became a bishop and got to

wear flowing red robes. Some pictures show him with a long white beard. His name day is 6 December, which is still the day on which people in many countries give presents. Nikólaos is also the patron saint of children, sailors, butchers, bakers and judges, to name but a few – so now you know what he keeps him busy for the rest of the year.

Modern Greeks

El Greco
El Greco is Spanish for 'the Greek' and it was the nickname given to a great 16th-century painter called Domenikos Theotokopoulos who was born in Crete, but spent much of his life in Spain. He painted mostly religious subjects and his work influenced many artists who came after him, including Picasso.

Spiridon Louis
When the first modern Olympic Games were held in Athens in 1896, someone had the bright idea of having a race in honour of Pheidippides's legendary 26-mile run from Marathon to Athens in 490 BC (which probably never happened at all, but so what?). The race was dubbed the marathon, and, just as in the original run, it began at 2 pm on a hot April afternoon. The runners were followed by doctors and nurses in horse-drawn carts, and also a couple of undertakers, in case anyone dropped down dead, as poor old Pheidippides is supposed to have done. After about an hour the Frenchman who had led from the start collapsed with heat exhaustion, and eventually Spiridon Louis, a former shepherd, postman and water-seller from Athens, who had trained by running alongside his mules, took the lead and won the first ever Olympic marathon event. The crowd went wild and Louis became a national hero.

Maria Callas

The Greek soprano Maria Callas was one of the most famous opera singers who ever lived. She had a beautiful singing voice, but was also a wonderful actress. Though she was born in New York City, in 1923, she moved back to Athens at the age of 13 with her Greek parents, before starting on her brilliant career. Unfortunately, Maria Callas had a rather sad personal life and died aged only 53. She is still revered as one of the greats of opera.

Nikos Kazantakis

One of the most important Greek writers of the 20th century, Kazantakis was born in Crete, but travelled very widely. His most famous novel, *The Life of Alexis Zorba*, was published in 1946 and was later made into a film, *Zorba the Greek*, starring the Greek actress Melina Mercouri and featuring lots of *bouzoúki* music.

Melina Mercouri

Melina Mercouri is a much-loved figure in modern Greece. A beautiful and glamorous actress, she fought against the military dictatorship in Greece between 1967 and 1974, and later became Minister of Culture in the Greek government. She campaigned for the return of the Elgin or Parthenon Marbles from Britain to Athens, and made sure that cultural affairs were always headline news in Greece. 'Culture is Greece's heavy industry', she once said. Mercouri also thought up the idea of having a different 'European City of Culture' every year, an event that unites all the countries of the European Union. She died in 1994.

Aristotle Onassis

In a country famed for its ships and shipbuilding, Aristotle Onassis is probably the most famous name in the business. Onassis came from a family of Greek refugees who were forced to leave their homes in the city of Smyrna in what is now Turkey. Onassis built up an international shipping business and became very wealthy indeed. He also founded the Greek national airline, Olympic. However, Onassis is often remembered today for the women in his life. He had a long love affair with the Greek opera singer Maria Callas, but then left her to marry Jacqueline Kennedy, widow of the US President John F. Kennedy.

Pyrros Dimas

Three times Olympic champion weightlifter, Pyrros Dimas was actually born in Albania, but emigrated to Greece in 1991. He won gold medals at the 1992 and 1996 Olympics, where he also set two world records. He then won a third gold at the Sydney Olympics in 2000. Dimas couldn't quite realise his dream of a record fourth gold medal at the Athens Olympics (he won the bronze). But he is still a hero in Greece, and was chosen to carry the Greek flag during the Athens opening ceremony.

Vangelis

Vangelis is a Greek composer, famous for his New Age and electronic music. He won an Oscar for his music for the film *Chariots of Fire* (1981) and he also composed the music for *Blade Runner*. Vangelis composed the anthem for the 2002 Football World Cup in Japan and Korea, and in 2001 a piece of his music called Mythodea was used by NASA as the theme for the Mars missions.

Stelios Haji-Ioannou

Born in Athens to parents from Cyprus, Stelios, as he prefers to be known, is a business entrepreneur and founder of the low-cost, 'no frills' airline easyJet, which he started in 1995 and which now flies to destinations all over Europe. Stelios has started lots of other companies under the 'easy' brand, including easyPizza, an online delivery service from which you can choose a pizza called 'El Stel'.

Fani Halkia

Fani Halkia, an athlete from Larissa, became a national heroine in Greece when she won the gold medal in the women's 400-metre hurdles at the 2004 Athens Olympics. Her lap of honour, draped in the Greek flag, was one of the highlights of the games.

Sophia Kokosalaki

The Greek designer Sophia Kokosalaki is a rising star in the fashion world. Born in Athens in 1974, she starting designing dresses when she was still a child because she didn't like the clothes she was made to wear! After gaining a Master's degree in fashion design in London, she started her own company. Her speciality is soft, flowing dresses, influenced by the draped garments of ancient Greece. Recently Sophia Kokosalaki spent a whole year designing more than 7,000 ceremonial costumes for the 2004 Athens Olympics. Fans of her clothes include Kate Moss and Courtney Love.

Theodoros Zagorakis

Zagorakis is the captain of the Greek national football team and the man who lifted the trophy after his team's victory in the final of the 2004 European Championships in Portugal. He was also named UEFA's Player of the Tournament. Zagorakis is from Kavala in the northwest of Greece. A mid-fielder, he now plays club football for the Italian side Bologna, but during his career he has also played for PAOK of Thessaloníki, AEK Athens and Leicester City in the UK. Zagorakis has won almost 100 caps for his country, more than any other player.

Food and Drink

Epicurus, a Greek philosopher who lived during the 3rd century BC, was famous for enjoying the pleasures of eating. To this day we still sometimes call someone who relishes good food an 'epicure'.

The philosophy of Epicurus is shared by most modern Greeks, who also love their food. But while overeating is leading to lots of health problems in the USA, the UK and many other countries, the Greeks are some of the healthiest people in the world. Most experts agree that what they eat is one of the main reasons why so many Greeks live to a ripe old age. Even though people in Greece, especially the young, now eat a lot of the same foods as you – pizza, pasta and hamburgers, for example – they still probably get more fresh food, fruit and vegetables in their diets. In general, Greeks are still fussy about where their food comes from and how fresh it is. Of all the peoples in the European Union, Greeks now eat the most meat, and the most cheese, even more than the French.

From the earliest days of its civilisation Greece has always produced a plentiful supply of wonderful food, both from the land and the sea. Greek specialities include fish (of course), chicken, lamb, fresh herbs, olives, fruit and nuts. Make sure you try as many of these things as you can when you are in Greece.

Typical Greek foods

Here are some typically Greek foods that you might want to sample when you are in Greece, either for lunch or supper, or any time in between!

☞ **Feta** is the most famous – and the oldest – of all the many different kinds of cheese in Greece. It is a white cheese made from goat's or occasionally sheep's milk, and has quite a strong salty taste, different from cheeses you might be used to. You could try it in the cheese pies that Greeks call *tirópites*, or in a traditional Greek salad.

☞ **Honey** is eaten a lot in Greece. Try drizzling some into a pot of Greek yoghurt for a tasty and very healthy breakfast.

☞ *Horiátiki saláta*, which means 'village salad' in Greek, is usually made with tomatoes, cucumber, onions, green pepper and black olives, with slices of *feta* cheese and a drizzle of olive oil on the top. It makes an excellent starter or side dish, and it is very good for you too.

☞ **Mezédes** are small starter dishes served with fresh bread. Some of these you may already know, such as *hoúmous* (a dip made with chickpeas) or *taramasálata* (dip made with fish roe). Make sure you also try *tsatzíki*, a delicious dip made with thick yoghurt, cucumber and garlic, or **melitzanosaláta**, made with aubergines. Two more delicious starters you could sample are *saganáki*, which is fried *feta* cheese sprinkled with lemon juice, and *dolmádes*, vine leaves stuffed with onions, rice and herbs.

☞ *Moussaká* is one of the most famous of all Greek dishes. It is made with layers of lamb mince, aubergine and white sauce, and topped with cheese.

☞ **Olives** are a bit of an acquired taste. If you think you don't like them, try them again when you're in Greece (you'll have plenty of chances) and just maybe you'll change your mind. You'll find both green and black olives in Greece – the green ones are those picked before they are ripe. Among the tastiest are Kalamáta black olives, which come from the town of the same name in the Peloponnese.

☞ *Pastítsio* is something you should try if you like pasta. It's another layered dish, this time with macaroni, lamb mince, cheese, cream and white sauce.

☞ *Souvlákia* contains cubes of meat (usually pork, sometimes beef), flavoured with lemon and herbs threaded onto a skewer, and then grilled. It's delicious with *tsatzíki*.

☞ *Stifádo* is a spiced beef stew with baby onions.

☞ **Yoghurt** in Greece tastes very different from the yoghurt you might find in the supermarket at home (even if the label says 'Greek yoghurt'!). It can be made from sheep's, goat's or cow's milk, and is thick and creamy.

Sweet stuff

Greeks don't go in much for puddings. If you're eating in a restaurant, you might be offered fruit, such as big refreshing wedges of watermelon, or grapes. One sweet the Greeks do love is *baklavá*, a very sticky concoction made with nuts and honey in filo pastry. Or you could try *hálva*, a sweet made with sesame seeds.

And to drink...

Greece produces plenty of wines, both red and white. One of the most famous is *retsína*, a wine that gets its distinctive taste and name because pine resin is added to it.

Oúzo is another Greek drink drunk by adults that tastes of aniseed. You might notice people drinking it because by itself it is clear, but when water is added it goes cloudy.

Of course, lots of soft drinks are also available in Greece, including fruit juices, mineral water and coke.

Eating out

Most Greeks are very sociable people who love going out. They eat out in restaurants – *tavernas* – with family and friends much more often than we do: twice a week is not unusual. Tavernas are rarely grand or expensive (otherwise people wouldn't be able to afford to eat out so often), but instead they are very informal and lively places, where children are always welcomed, and there are usually tables outside. The cooking is simple, but the ingredients are almost always fresh and wholesome, but don't forget to talk lots as well!

In villages there is usually a coffee house, called a *kafenió*. It's also a kind of social club, where groups of men (and sometimes, though much less often, women) get together to discuss the latest news and gossip, read the papers, have a nap or play cards and backgammon. The coffee is strong and served in small white cups along with a cold glass of water.

Breakfast

Many Greeks do not bother with breakfast, but make do with a cup of strong, sweet coffee, served in small, white china cups from a pot called a *briki*. But if you're hungry and want to eat a traditional (and very healthy!) Greek breakfast, forget breakfast cereal and try a bowl of thick Greek yoghurt, with some honey on the top, or some fresh fruit. Delicious!

Mid-morning

By this time many Greeks are getting a little peckish, and so they might head to the bakery (*foúrnos*) to pick up a delicious cheese pie (*tirópita*) or perhaps a spinach one (*spanakópita*). Both are made with crunchy filo pastry.

Lunch

In general, Greeks eat later than you might be used to. Lunch is usually taken between 2 pm and 3.30 pm. It used to be the main meal of the day, but now this is often taken in the evening instead, because more people are now out at work all day. Long lunches with wine are still common, though, especially at weekends and during the holidays. Afterwards many Greeks have an afternoon nap, or *mesiméri*, to avoid the heat, waking up around 6 or 7 pm for a swim and an ice cream!

Supper

Again, supper happens later than you're probably used to at home: Greeks generally sit down to eat any time from 9 pm to 11.30 pm, and meals can go on into the small hours. You might find that your fellow diners break into song or dance, and that you are watching a Greek cabaret. But don't expect to see any flying crockery. Smashing plates in praise of musicians or dancers replaced an earlier way of showing approval by throwing knives into the floor at the performer's feet. Plate-smashing is now officially off the menu in most restaurants in Greece: in fact, these days you need a licence to do it. Now people throw flowers instead.

By the way, when you've finished your meal and you need to get the bill, ask for *to logariasmó*.

Greek Myths

The twelve Olympian gods and goddesses

There were many Greek gods and goddesses, but the most important were the 12 who lived on Mount Olympus. The ancient Greeks believed that their gods had extraordinary powers, while looking just like ordinary people. Many Greek myths show the gods behaving just like people too – quarrelling, fighting and falling in love. The 12 Olympians were all members of one big, unhappy family. There were four older gods:

☞ Zeus, ruler of the gods and god of the weather.

☞ Hera, his wife, goddess of women and marriage.

☞ Demeter, Zeus's sister, goddess of crops and fertility.

☞ Poseidon, brother of Zeus, god of the sea, earthquakes and horses.

and eight of Zeus's many children:

☞ Aphrodite, goddess of love and beauty.

☞ Apollo, god of the Sun, truth, music, poetry, dance and healing.

☞ Ares, god of war.

☞ Hephaestos, god of fire, volcanoes, blacksmiths and craftsmen.

☞ Artemis, goddess of the moon, wild animals and

childbirth.

- ☞ Athena, goddess of war, wisdom and art (and of Athens).
- ☞ Dionysus, god of wine, vegetation and parties!
- ☞ Hermes, god of travel, business, weights and measures and sport.

Here are a few weird and wonderful Greek myths that you may not know.

In the beginning...

At the beginning of time Uranus ('Heaven') and Gaia ('Earth') had 12 sons and 12 daughters. They were known as the Titans. One day one of the Titans, Cronos, seized the throne from his father. Uranus cursed him, saying, 'One day *your* son will take power from *you*.' Desperate to make sure that this did not happen, Cronos swallowed all his own children, except for the one who was still in his wife Rhea's belly at the time. Rhea ran away and gave birth to a boy in secret, naming him Zeus. When Zeus grew up, he rescued his brothers and sisters from Cronos's stomach, and beat his father and the other Titans in a war for control of the universe. Zeus then divided up the world, drawing lots with his brothers and sisters – Poseidon, Hades, Hestia, Demeter and Hera – to decide who would get what.

Liar, liar, Troy on fire

Cassandra was a princess of Troy. When she was a child the god Apollo fell in love with her and gave her the gift of prophecy: that is, the ability to see into the future. From that day on Cassandra heard voices telling her what was going to happen, which, for a while at least, proved a very useful party trick. When she was 16, however, Apollo came back to claim Cassandra as his wife. She refused to marry him, so he gave her a second gift, by way of revenge – and the gift was disbelief. Now, every time Cassandra predicted the future, no one believed her. She told her mother and father that Troy would lose the Trojan War, and that they would all be taken prisoner by the Greeks. Everyone laughed at her. She even warned them about the Trojan horse, telling them that it was a trick by the Greeks to get into the city. But again no one listened. After 10 years of war the Greeks conquered Troy, just as Cassandra had predicted. Her parents died and Cassandra was taken into slavery.

Death mask of Agamemnon, leader of the Greek army at Troy

I hear thunder

Back in ancient Greece the time came for a man named Sisyphus to die, but he didn't want to, so he hatched a plan with his wife Merope. After Death came for Sisyphus and took him down to the Underworld, Merope dumped his body and carried on with her life as if nothing had happened. Down in the Underworld Sisyphus protested to Hades, the god in charge, saying that it wasn't right that Merope was behaving like this, and please could he just pop back to sort her out. Hades agreed, on condition that Sisyphus returned straightaway. Of course, when he got back to Earth Merope welcomed him with open arms. Their cunning plan to cheat Death had been a great success and Sisyphus had no intention of returning. But the gods got the better of Sisyphus in the end. As an eternal punishment he was ordered to roll a huge rock up a mountain and then down the other side. The rock is so heavy, however, that, as soon as Sisyphus gets it to the top, it rolls back down to the bottom and he has to start all over again. Some say that the sound we hear as thunder is really Sisyphus's rock rolling back down the mountain.

Halcyon days

Zephyrus, the West Wind, had a beautiful daughter called Halcyone, who fell in love with a human being called Ceyx, who was a sailor. One day, however, Zephyrus blew too hard by accident. Ceyx's ship sank and he was drowned. Zephyrus tried to comfort his daughter, but she was distraught, so Zephyrus appealed to Zeus to bring Ceyx back to life. Zeus refused, so Halcyone said that she would rather become a mortal human being and be with Ceyx than stay a goddess and give him up. So Zeus threw two handfuls of magic feathers over Halcyone and the soul of Ceyx. The next moment two kingfishers appeared, dressed in all the turquoise colours of the sea. Halcyone and Ceyx were together again. Once a year, it is said, Halcyone builds a nest of fishbones that floats on the sea, and lays her eggs in it. She sits on the nest for 14 days, and while she does so her father Zephyrus tiptoes around her and blows not a breath of wind. Sailors call this fortnight of calm the 'halcyon days'. And there are still plenty of kingfishers around to this day.

Wreaths of honour

Daphne was a nymph, daughter of the river god Pineos. The god Apollo fell in love with her (he fell in love a lot, did Apollo) and chased her through the woods. Just as he caught up with her Daphne said a prayer to her father to save her. Pineos heard her just in time, and turned Daphne into a laurel tree. But Apollo still loved her, and declared the laurel sacred, and his special tree. Laurel wreaths have been used ever since as a mark of honour for heroes and poets – and the Greek word for 'laurel' is still *daphne*.

I've got my eyes on you

Hera, the wife of Zeus, was very jealous. She had good reason to be, as Zeus fell in love with lots of other women. So that she would always know what he was up to, Hera created a giant monster called Argus, a dragon-like creature with 100 eyes. The 50 pairs of eyes all over his body took it in turns to close in sleep, so the monster was always awake. However, Zeus asked his son Hermes, the messenger of the gods, to tell stories and play music to lull Argus to sleep. The plan worked and, as Argus slumbered, Hermes killed him with his sword. Hera wasn't to be outdone, however. She cast a spell over the dying Argus, and he was transformed into a beautiful bird with iridescent feathers of green, purple and blue, and a fan-like tail with an eye on the tip of every feather. Yes, that's right, he became a peacock. And to this day the eyes on the tail of a peacock never close.

Festivals and National Celebrations

Every day is a festival day somewhere in Greece! Feast days are celebrated with great enthusiasm by both young and old, and are marked by family gatherings, special meals, and a lot of noise and excitement. Most festivals in Greece come from the traditions of the Greek Orthodox Church. It's worth remembering that the celebrations for a lot of the big festivals start the night before, and go on all night and into the next day. So it's no good turning up in the afternoon – you might find that you've missed the party.

Easter

Easter is the most important festival in Greece and is taken much more seriously than almost anywhere else in Europe. It is still a very spiritual time for most Greeks, even those who are not particularly religious. The date of Easter in the Orthodox Church is different from that in the Catholic and Protestant Churches, and usually falls at least a week later. It is a time of fasting, processions and dancing.

Easter begins with Holy Week, when almost everyone fasts and drops into church, even if only for a few minutes to hear special prayers being said. On Good Friday evening an *epitáfios* or funeral bier to represent the one which carried the crucified Jesus, lavishly decorated with flowers, leaves each church and is paraded solemnly through the streets. In some places, such as Crete, for example, people burn effigies of

Judas Iscariot, the betrayer of Jesus.

A midnight service is held on Holy Saturday to celebrate the resurrection of Jesus, and it is a very moving occasion. On the stroke of midnight all the lights in the church go out before the priest appears from behind the altar carrying a candle. Then other candles are lit, church bells ring, fireworks explode and people leave church, carrying their candles and saying to each other '*Christós Anésti*' ('Christ has risen'). The worshippers take their candles home still lit, as they are said to bring good fortune to the house if they arrive still burning. Some people make the sign of the cross with the flame on their front doors, leaving a black smudge visible for the rest of the year.

Early on Easter Sunday morning the Lenten fast is traditionally broken with a meal of *mayerítsa*, or 'resurrection soup', made with lamb offal, rice, dill and lemon. The rest of the lamb is roasted on a spit for the traditional Easter Sunday lunch, and the celebrations continue for the rest of the day.

Greeks do have Easter eggs, but traditionally they are real eggs, not chocolate ones, hard-boiled and painted red on Easter Thursday. They are sometimes baked into twisted, sweet loaves of sweet bread and given out on Easter Sunday. People rap their eggs against their friends' eggs, and the owner of the last uncracked egg is considered lucky! Egg salad, anyone?

In the week leading up to Easter Sunday you should wish people a happy Easter

– '*Kaló Páskha*'. On Easter Sunday itself you say '*Khrónia pollá*', which means 'Many happy returns'.

On Good Friday, girls who live in the town of Leonídio in the Peloponnese gather wildflowers and compete to make the most beautiful *epitáfios* or funeral bier for the dead Jesus. Everyone goes to church on Easter Sunday, just as they do all over Greece, but in Leonídio, at the moment of the Resurrection, more than 500 huge balloons with flames in baskets beneath are released, and they fly straight up towards the stars.

Name days

Most Greeks are named after an Orthodox saint, so traditionally they celebrate the name day of their saint, instead of birthdays (though nowadays, many children celebrate their birthdays as well, lucky things). Friends and families drop by on your name day with small presents, and it is traditional to give them cakes and refreshments in return.

Here are some common Greek names and their name days (*giortí*):

☞ Yiórgos	23 April
☞ Konstandínos	21 May
☞ Eleni	21 May
☞ Pétros	29 June
☞ Pávlos	29 June

☞ Marína	17 July
☞ Yiannis	6 August
☞ Maria	15 August
☞ Dhimítrios	27 October
☞ Níkos	6 December
☞ Spyrídon	12 December

Saints' days

As well as the main festivals of the Orthodox Church, each local church in Greece has its special saint's day, known as a *panegýri*. This is celebrated with church services, picnics, music and dancing. Many Greeks who have moved away from their home villages and towns return to them to celebrate the *panegýri*. The eating, drinking and merriment often last for days. You might be lucky and stumble upon a local saint's day festival when you are in Greece. Some of the most important – and the strangest – are described below.

New Year's Day (Protohroniá)

The first of January is the feast day of Saint Basil, and is celebrated with church services and the baking of a special loaf of bread, the *vassilópitta*, in which a coin has been baked. The person who finds it is said to have good luck throughout the year.

Epiphany (6 January)

On Epiphany, *Ta Fóta,* priests in towns and villages close to rivers or to the sea bless the waters by throwing a cross into them. The young men of the town then dive into the water and try to retrieve the cross. Brrrrr!

Gynaecocratía (8 January)

Gynaecocratía or Ladies' Day is celebrated in a few rural

villages in Thrace, a region in the northeastern corner of Greece. On this day every year women take over men's jobs for the day. This basically means that they go to the local café to drink coffee, play cards and enjoy themselves until the early hours, while the men stay at home and do the housework. If any man dares to show his face, he gets a bucket of water thrown over him. Good on you, girls!

Lent and 'Clean Monday'

Lent, the period of 40 days leading up to Easter, is traditionally a time of fasting in Christian churches. This custom of eating and drinking less than usual is still widely observed in Greece. Before Lent there are three weeks of fun when the pre-Lenten carnivals are held, with parades, costume parties, and lots of eating and drinking while people still have the chance. Some of the biggest celebrations take place in the town of Pátra in the Peloponnese. On the island of Skýros in the Sporades a famous goat dance takes place. It's an ancient pagan ritual in which people wear shepherds' outfits, goatskin masks and lots of bells, and dance around the narrow streets.

The last Sunday of carnival is followed by the first day of Lent, 'Clean Monday', or, in Greek, *Katharí Deftéra*. It is so

called because traditionally on this day housewives cleaned all their kitchen utensils to get rid of all traces of food before the Lenten fast. Nowadays it's more often a day for a family picnic at which a special Clean Monday loaf of bread called a *lagana* is eaten. It's a long, flat loaf with rounded corners and lots of sesame seeds. It is also traditional for children to fly kites on Clean Monday.

Independence Day and the Annunciation (25 March)

This day is both a religious and a national holiday, when everyone has the day off. There are military parades and dancing to celebrate the beginning of the Greek revolt against Turkish rule in 1821. There are also church services to honour the Annunciation, when Mary was given the news that she was to become the mother of Jesus.

The Feast of St George (23 April)

The feast of Saint George (*Ayios Yiorgos*) is a big rural celebration in Greece, because he is the patron saint of shepherds. There is much feasting and dancing at shrines and churches dedicated to him. At Aráchova in central

Greece, north of Delphi, there is a three-day festival that ends with the village's elderly men racing each other in traditional dress.

Protomayá (May Day, 1 May)

May Day is a great holiday for people living in towns and cities. Traditionally on this day they make for the countryside to picnic, returning with bunches of wild flowers. Wreaths are hung on doorways and balconies.

The Feast of St Konstandinos and St Eleni (21 May)

Firewalking is the order of this day in certain villages in Macedonia in northern Greece. Every year people dance barefoot over hot coals to the music of lyres and drums, while holding aloft icons of *Ayíos Konstandinos* and *Agía Eleni*. This strange ceremony commemorates the time in the 13th century when the church where the icons were kept caught fire. The villagers heard the icons 'groaning', so they ran to rescue them. Strangely enough, no one was burned. Since then, the tradition goes, villagers have been able to walk over fire without coming to any harm.

St John's Day (24 June)

On the feast day of St John (*Ayíos Ioánnis*) in the town of Chaniá on Crete a custom called *Klidonas* takes place. The unmarried women of the town fetch water from the well and empty it into pots and buckets, into which they have also put a personal item of value. The containers are left outside overnight, and, so it is said, the women dream of their future husbands.

The Transfiguration (6 August)

The day on which Jesus appeared in a vision with Elijah and Moses (the *Metamórfos)* is celebrated with food fights on the Dodecanese island of Chálki. If you want to join in, the favourite things to chuck around are eggs, flour and squid ink.

The Assumption of the Virgin Mary (15 August)

On the important feast of the Assumption of the Virgin Mary (*tis Panayías*), people traditionally return to their home villages, so it's not a good time to be trying to find a room. Even some Greeks sleep in the streets! The island of Tínos in the Cyclades is home to a famous icon of the Virgin Mary that is said to have miraculous healing powers. On 15 August every year the islanders carry the statue down to the harbour over the heads of the faithful.

The Birth of the Virgin Mary (8 September)

This is an important feast day in the Orthodox Church. It is also the anniversary of the Battle of the Straits off the island of Spétses in 1822, during the Greek War of Independence. It is marked on the island by a re-enactment of the battle, followed by a big party and a fireworks display.

Óhi Day (28 October)

This national holiday is celebrated with parades, folk-dancing and speeches to commemorate Prime Minister Ioannis Metaxas's one-word reply to the Italian dictator Mussolini in 1940 when he wanted to send Italian troops into Greece: '*Óhi*!' ('No!'). Actually, what he really said was, 'This means war.' And it did.

The Feast of St Nicholas (6 December)

St Nicholas (*Ayíos Nikólaos*) is a very important saint in Greece because he's the patron of seafarers.

Christmas Day

While it isn't as important as Easter, Christmas is still a big religious festival. In recent years Greeks have started to adopt many of features of the western Christmas, such as decorations, Christmas trees and gifts. However, 26 December is not Boxing Day, but *Sýnaxis tis Panayías*, or the Gathering of the Virgin's Entourage, no less.

New Year's Eve

New Year's Eve is traditionally a day for carol singing and for playing cards.

A Little Bit of Sport

The two sports that Greeks are most fanatical about are basketball and football (meaning soccer, of course!), though many other sports are popular too. 2004 will probably go down in history as the most important year for sport in Greece since the ancient Greeks had the idea of starting the Olympics. Not only did the Greek football team win the European Championships, to the surprise of the whole world, but, later in the summer, Athens hosted the Olympic Games, an event that the whole country had been getting ready for for years.

Basketball

Basketball was introduced to Greece less than 100 years ago, in 1918, when some bright spark grabbed some friends, took two chairs, hung them upside down on two walls and used a football for the first basketball match anywhere in Greece. Since then the sport has become very popular. The Greek basketball team is one of the best in Europe and won the European Championship in 1987. Some of the leading basketball clubs in Greece are owned by the big football teams and share a name with them – for example,

Panathinaikós, Olympiakos, AEK Athens and Aris.

The Kallimármaro Stadium in Athens was the setting for a unique world basketball record. On 4 April 1968 AEK Athens won the European Basketball Cup, beating Slavia Prague, in front of 60,000 spectators, the largest crowd ever to attend a basketball match.

The Spartathlon

When John Foden, a wing commander in the British RAF, read the Greek historian Herodotus's story of how Pheidippides ran the 260 km from Athens to Sparta, he was so inspired that he decided to try it himself. He ran the route in 36 hours and in 1983 he set up the first Spartathlon race. This ultra-marathon now takes place in September every year, starting at the gate of the Acropolis in Athens. Competitors have a maximum of 36 hours to finish the race. The current record for the men's event is 20 hours; for the women's it is 28 hours. And the prize for winner? An olive branch and a glass of river water.

Football/Soccer

Even before the national team won Euro 2004, football was hugely popular in Greece. Every town has its own football team and even small villages often play matches against each other. The biggest and most widely supported football clubs in Greece are:

☞ Panathinaikós, an Athens team who play in green and white, and are named after the goddess Athena.

- ☞ AEK Athens, who play in black and yellow.
- ☞ Olympiakós of Piraeus, who play in red and white.
- ☞ PAOK from Thessaloníki, who play in black and white.

The Greek football champions for 2003–04 were Panathinaikós. For the previous seven years the champions had been Olympiakós. So it made a nice change… unless you happened to be an Olympiakós fan of course.

Sixteen countries competed in Euro 2004 in Portugal to find the best national football team in Europe. Few people thought that Greece stood any chance of winning, especially as the team had never won a single match in a major competition before. Against all expectations, the Greek team started by winning the first game of the tournament against the hosts, Portugal, and went on to qualify for the quarterfinals, where they beat the tournament holders, France. After beating the Czech Republic in the semifinals they met Portugal again in the final on 4 July in Lisbon. The final score was 1–0 to Greece. The result broke Portuguese hearts, but almost the whole of Greece went wild with joy. Thousands of people spilled out onto the streets of Athens and elsewhere, in a huge show of national rejoicing. The Greek players became national heroes overnight, and so did the German team coach, Otto Rehhagel, who earned himself the nickname King Otto. The

Greek Prime Minister at the time, George Papandréou, captured the mood of celebration when he said: 'This beautiful occasion, a dream that we still cannot believe has come true, has raised Greece very high.'

Greece's Euro 2004 victory counted as one of the sport's biggest-ever upsets, and sent the team skyrocketing up the FIFA World Football rankings, from 35th before the tournament to 14th afterwards. This was the biggest-ever jump by any team in a single month. The triumph was also rated top in the list of '10 outstanding sports events' for 2004 published by the international news agency Associated Press. Greece won because they had a fantastic defence, only conceding four goals in the whole tournament. At the same time they took the so-called bigger teams by surprise by being very effective on the counter-attack. All this was achieved without mega-star players or a manager with a huge six-figure salary. It just shows you how far determination and team spirit can get you.

The Athens Olympics

In 2004, for the first time since 1896, the Olympic Games were held in Greece, the country where they were invented. Most of the events took place in Athens, where preparations for the Games started years in advance. A new international airport was built, as well as new metro and tram links, and many roads were improved and widened.

The Greeks built a huge sports complex, including four Olympic-size stadiums. The biggest of these, crowned with a glass and steel dome, became the main athletics venue, and was the stage for the opening ceremony and the lighting of the Olympic flame. An Olympic village was also built to house the 16,000 athletes and officials taking part in both the main Olympics and the Paralympics, which followed in September.

Before the start of the Games there were rumours that Greece was struggling to have everything ready in time. In the end, pretty much everything was done in time for the opening ceremony on 13 August.

The ceremonial lighting of the Olympic flame had taken place on 25 March at Olympia. For the first time ever the flame went on a world tour to former Olympic host cities and other large cities, passing through the hands of 10,000 torchbearers, before returning to Greece. Nikolaos Kaklamanakis, a Greek sailing champion who won a gold medal at the 1996 Olympics, did the honours and lit the huge flame in a bowl in the Athens Olympic stadium.

202 nations from around the world took part in the Athens Olympics, and 11,099 individual athletes participated in 301 events in 28 sports. Each medal-winner was crowned with a *kotinos*, a wreath made of olive leaves, just as they were at the ancient Olympics. Greece itself won a respectable total of 16 medals (six gold, six silver and four bronze).

Around 3.5 million people travelled to the Athens Olympics from around the world. Many said that they had witnessed the greatest spectacle on Earth, helping Greece to make headlines all over the world, for the second time in one summer!

Odds and Ends

Marbles

Greece and Britain generally get along well together, but there is one subject they disagree strongly about, and that is who should have the Elgin Marbles. This has nothing to with the small glass balls you roll along the ground. The Elgin Marbles are actually several large sculptures made of marble that Lord Elgin, a British ambassador, removed from the Parthenon in Athens in the early 19th century and brought back to Britain. At the time the Ottomans were in charge in Greece, and they were quite happy to sell them to Lord Elgin. Today many people in Britain think that the Marbles are still best looked after by the very experienced curators at the British Museum, where they remain on display to visitors. However, most Greeks – who funnily enough, prefer to call them the Parthenon Marbles – believe passionately that they belong in Athens. They have been running a long campaign for their return, and have even left space for them in a new museum, but so far the British government has refused to budge, and so in the British Museum the Parthenon Marbles remain.

It's all Greek to me

Someone, somewhere, once said that if all the words of Greek origin were suddenly removed from the world's dictionaries, all intelligent conversation would come to an end. Amazingly, around 10 per cent of the words in the English language today have their origins in Classical Greek. There's an expression: 'It's all Greek to me', which means, 'I don't understand it.' But every time you use the words below, you are speaking a little bit of Greek, and probably a little bit that you understand very well!

☞ *alphabet*: from the names of the first two letters of the Greek alphabet, *alpha* and *beta.*

☞ *Bible*: from the word *biblia*, which means 'books'. The Greek word comes from the Phoenician city of Byblos, which produced papyrus, the stuff they used to make the paper out of which books were made.

☞ **dinosaur**: one you might know already, from two words – *deinos*, meaning 'terrible', and *sauros*, meaning 'lizard'.

☞ **echo**: In Greek mythology Echo was the name of a nymph. Hera, the wife of Zeus, put a curse on her, which meant that she could only talk by repeating what others had just said. So from Echo we get our word 'echo'.

☞ **galaxy**: from the word *gala*, which means milk. Well, you've heard of the Milky Way, haven't you? And now you know why that chocolate bar is called Galaxy too.

☞ **helicopter**: from two words – *helix*, meaning 'spiral', and *pteron*, meaning 'wing'.

☞ **idea:** from the word *idein*, meaning 'to see'.

☞ **lyric**: The ancient Greek word *lyrikos* meant a song sung to the tune of a lyre, an ancient stringed instrument. Now, of course, lyrics are the words of any song.

☞ **panic**: This comes from Pan, the Greek god of pastures, flocks, and shepherds, who is supposed to have struck fear into the enemies of his subjects. Panic even.

☞ **telephone**: from two words – *tele*, meaning 'far away', and *phone*, meaning 'voice'.

☞ **zoo**: from the word *zoon*, meaning 'animal'. From *zoon* we also get the word 'zodiac'.

114

Know your columns

Ancient Greek buildings, especially the temples, had columns to hold the roof up. They come in three different styles, and it's quite fun to be able to recognise which is which. The easiest way to do this is by looking at the tops of the columns, which are called the 'capitals'

☞ Doric columns are the simplest columns and have plain capitals.

☞ Ionic columns have a capital in the shape of a spiral scroll on two sides.

☞ Corinthian columns have capitals decorated with carvings of leaves on all four sides.

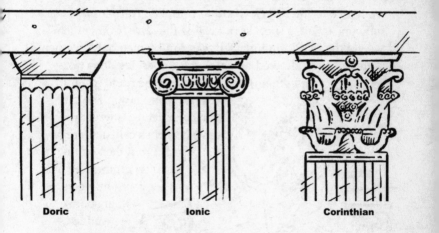

Doric   Ionic   Corinthian

Copycat buildings

In cities all over the world there are buildings that look like those in ancient Greece. They might have columns, or friezes, or even statues. The reason they look so similar is that over the centuries many architects have admired the way the ancient Greeks designed buildings and decided to pinch their ideas. This copied style of architecture is often

115

called 'neo-classical'. There are loads of examples: two of the most famous are the British Museum and the National Gallery in London. In the US the White House and the Capitol Building in Washington DC were both built in neo-classical styles.

The Olympic Games

Most ancient Greeks were keen on keeping fit. To prove it they spent a lot of time running races, and in 776 BC the first Olympic Games were held on the plain of Olympia in the Peloponnese. The games were dedicated to the god Zeus and, while they were in progress, peace was declared between all warring cities. Athletes travelled to Olympia from all over the Greek world to compete. At first there was only one event, a short sprint called the *stade* (from which we get the word 'stadium'). It was run by men only (women were not even allowed to watch the games, let alone take part in them) and they ran in the nude (well it was hot, you know). The winners received a wreath of olive branches called a *kotinos*. From then on the Olympics were held every four years. Other sports were added, including more running races (some in full armour), wrestling, boxing, races on horseback and chariot races. In the pentathlon athletes had to compete

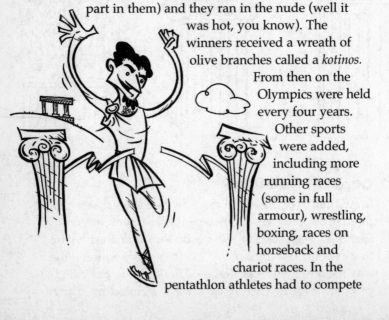

in five events – long jump, javelin-throwing, discus-throwing, racing on foot and horse-racing – to find the best all rounder. The most ferocious event was probably the *pankration*, a combination of boxing and wrestling in which almost anything, short of eye-gouging and biting, was allowed. Apparently, a good tactic was to break all your opponent's fingers and then finish him off when he was helpless to fight back.

Umpires made sure that there was fair play. Instead of whistles they carried sticks to whack any athlete who didn't abide by the rules. There were also large fines for cheating.

A flame was lit at each Olympics in Ancient Greece, which burned throughout the games to symbolise the death and rebirth of Greek heroes. It's a tradition that is followed today. The Olympics weren't just a sporting event, they were a bit of pagan festival as well. As well as all that running around, there were also religious ceremonies, sacrifices and banquets.

The Olympics were banned in AD 394 by the Byzantine Emperor Theodosius II, and didn't happen again until 1896, when a Frenchman, Baron de Coubertin, had the bright idea of bringing them back. The first modern Olympic Games were held in Athens. Quite right too.

The science bit

The ancient Greeks were amazingly advanced when it came to science. They drew maps of the Earth and of the sky. A man called Heracleitus spotted the planets and listed them in their correct order from the Earth. Someone called Eratosthenes calculated that the circumference of the Earth was 40,000 kilometres. Amazingly, he was only 67 kilometres out! In 275 BC Aristarchus of Sámos suggested that the sun was the centre of the solar system (though most people didn't believe him).

Not long afterwards, in 212 BC, the famous inventor Archimedes (the one who jumped out of his bathtub shouting *Eureka)* came up with a brilliant way of using solar power to defeat your enemies. When the Roman fleet was sent to attack his home town of Syracuse, he told some soldiers to polish their bronze shields until they could see their faces in them. He then got them to stand on the quayside in a curved formation to create a huge mirror and position it so as to concentrate the sun's rays onto the Roman fleet. The ships promptly caught fire and that was the end of the attack.

All the world's a stage

Going to see a play in ancient Greece was a quite different experience from a night out in the West End today. Greek theatres were open-air and semi-circular. The front part of the acting area was called the *orchestra*, and the stage or *skene* (from which we get the word 'scenery') was the raised bit behind it. During a play a group of about 15 people called the chorus stood in the *orchestra* and spoke together, telling the story and making comments on what was happening. The actors, meanwhile, stood on the stage and spoke the lines of the main characters. All the actors were men, who changed character by wearing different masks. The masks had hair attached and could represent male or female characters, young or old. Both tragedies and comedies were performed. Tragedies usually retold old myths about the gods and heroes, and they often turned out unhappily. Comedies were funny and told everyday stories.

The Greek flag

The national flag dates from the time of the Greek War of Independence against the Ottoman Empire in the early 19th century. It has nine horizontal blue and white stripes, and a white Greek cross on a blue background in the top left-hand corner. The stripes are supposed to stand for the nine syllables of the Greek revolutionaries' motto during the war, *Eleutheria e Thanatos*, which means 'Freedom or Death'. The striped pattern was chosen to look like the waves that surround the shores of Greece – if you see the flag fluttering on a windy day, those straight lines become wavy like the sea. The Greek cross symbolises the Greek Orthodox Church, of course. Finally, the colours: blue for the sea and white for the restless waves. Or maybe it's the clouds. Some people think that the colours match the uniforms worn by Greek sailors during the War of Independence. Whichever it is, it's a gorgeous flag.

The Greek national anthem

The Guinness Book of Records lists the Greek national anthem as the longest in the world – the full version has 158 stanzas or verses. The anthem, which is called *Ymnos eis tin Eleftherian* or 'Ode to Freedom', was written by a 19th-century poet called Dionysios Solomos, who came from the island of Zákynthos and was inspired by the Greek struggle for independence against Ottoman rule. Disappointingly, there isn't room for the full record-breaking version, but it was translated from the Greek by none other than Rudyard Kipling, author of *The Jungle Book*:

Confusing royal connections

In 1947 Queen Elizabeth II, who was then still Princess Elizabeth, married Prince Philip, who then became the Duke of Edinburgh. And very British he is too. However, he was actually born on Corfu into a different reigning royal family altogether. Impressively, Philip is closely related to the kings of Greece. But here's the confusing bit. He isn't actually Greek at all. His grandfather was William George, a son of the King of Denmark who was invited to take the Greek throne as George I in 1863. Are you still with me? Philip's uncle and cousins were on and off the throne for years while the Greek people tried to decide if they wanted a king or not. They finally voted to abolish the monarchy in 1974.

Emergency
Phrases

Try to pronounce the words just as they are written here. You'll notice that almost every word has an accent marked over a letter. This is because in Greek it's important to put the stress or emphasis in the right place in the word, otherwise you could completely change the meaning!

If you do get stuck, remember that lots of Greeks speak English. Not many visitors make the effort to speak their language in return. So it really is worth having a go: the Greeks will love you for it!

Greetings/Basics

Hello/Hi	*Yía sou (informal)*
	Yía sas (formal, or if you're talking to more than one person)
Good morning	*Kalí méra*
Good afternoon/evening	*Kalí spéra*
Goodbye	*Yía sou/Adío*
Yes	*Né*
No	*Óhi*
Please	*Parakaló*
Thank you	*Efharistó*
Excuse me	*Parakaló/Mípos*
Sorry	*signómi*
Pardon? (I didn't hear you)	*Oríste?*
today	*símera*
tonight	*apópse*
tomorrow	*ávrio*
yesterday	*khthés*
What?	*Tí?*
Where?	*Poú?*

When?	*Póte?*
Why?	*Yiatí?*
How?	*Pós?*

Getting to Know People

I am English (girl)	*Ime Anglidha*
I am English (boy)	*Ime Anglos*
I am American (girl)	*Ime Amerikana*
I am American (boy)	*Ime Amerikanós*
I am on holiday	*Káno tis diakopés mou*
I don't understand (Greek)	*Dhén katalavéno (ellinká)*
Do you speak English?	*Miláte anglká?*
I speak a bit of Greek	*Miláo ellinká lígho*
What's your name?	*Pós se léne?*
My name is …	*Mé léne…*
How old are you?	*Póso hronón ise?*
I am eight/nine/ten/	*Ime okhtó/ennéa/dhéka/*
eleven/twelve years old	*éndheka/dhódheka*
I am from England/America	*Ime apó tin Anglía/Amerikí/*
/Wales/Scotland	*Wália/Skótia*
How are you?	*Tí kánis?*
I'm fine	*Kalá íme*
And you?	*Ké essís?*
Where do you live?	*Pou ménis?*
I live in London/New York	*Méno sto Londíno/Néa Yórky*
What's new?	*Tí néa?*
What time is it?	*Ti óra íne?*
Let's go	*Páme*
See you soon	*Kalí andhámosi*
Do you have a PlayStation™?	*Éhis PlayStation™?*

Getting Around

entrance	*ísothos*
exit	*éxothos*
right/Turn right	*thexiá/Strípste thexiá*
left/Turn left	*aristerá/Strípste aristerá*

straight on	*eftheía*
near	*kontá*
far	*makriá*
Where is …?	*Poú íne…?*
Where is the toilet?	*Poú íne i toualéta?*
hotel	*xenodohío*
beach	*paralía*
sea	*thálassa*
castle	*kástro*
museum	*mousío*
church	*eklisía*
town square	*platía*
station	*stathmós*
swimming pool	*pisína*

Shopping

I would like…	*Tha íthela…*
How much is it?/are they?	*Póso kánei?/kánoun?*
supermarket	*soupermárket*
butcher's	*kreopoleío*
baker's	*foúrnos*
chemist's	*farmakeío*
cake shop	*zacharoplasteío*
post office	*tahidromío*
stamps	*gramatósima*
market	*agorá*
open	*anikhtó*
closed	*klistó*

Food and drink

breakfast	*proinó*
lunch	*mesimerianó*
dinner	*vradinó*
menu	*katálogo*
glass	*potíri*
bottle	*boukáli*

I am a vegetarian	*Ime hortofághos*
The bill, please	*To logarisamó, parakaló*
ice cream	*pagató*
orange juice	*hymó portokáli*
water	*neró*
Coke	*Kóka-kóla*
lemonade	*lemonádha*
hot chocolate	*zestí sokoláta*
bread	*psomí*
honey	*méli*
sugar	*záhari*
cheese	*tyrí*
yoghurt	*yiaoúrti*
olives	*elíes*

Other phrases

I am hungry	*Pinó*
I am thirsty	*Thipsó*
I am tired	*Ime kourasménos/kourasméni*
Great / Fine	*Mía hará!*
Bon voyage	*Kaló taxidhi*

Numbers

1	*énas/éna/mía*	13	*dhekatrís*
2	*dhío*	14	*dhekatésseris*
3	*trís/tría*	20	*íkosi*
4	*tésseris/téssera*	21	*íkosi éna*
5	*pénde*	30	*triánda*
6	*éxi*	40	*saránda*
7	*eptá*	50	*penínda*
8	*okhtó*	60	*exínda*
9	*ennéa*	70	*evdhomínda*
10	*dhéka*	80	*ogdhónda*
11	*éndheka*	90	*enenínda*
12	*dhódehka*	100	*ekató*

Good Books

Fiction books

Shadow of the Minotaur, Alan Gibbons (Orion)
A novel that takes you into the world of Greek mythology in an unusual and thrilling way, when Phoenix, the main character, finds himself inside a virtual reality computer game, playing the part of Theseus as he fights the Minotaur.

The Odyssey, Homer (Oxford University Press)
Why not have a go at reading a real Greek classic? Homer's poems are easier to follow than you might think, and the story of Odysseus's ten-year voyage home from fighting in the Trojan War is action-packed.

The Orchard Book of Greek Myths, Geraldine McCaughrean, (Orchard)
Retellings of the most famous Greek myths, together with a few more unusual ones.

Non-Fiction books

Horrible Histories: The Groovy Greeks, Terry Deary (Scholastic)
This book gets down to the nitty-gritty about life in Ancient Greece, with plenty of gruesome Greek facts.

My Family and Other Animals, Gerald Durrell (Penguin)
All about his wonderful childhood on Corfu in the 1930s, with his crazy family and a menagerie of animals, including toads, tortoises, bats and scorpions.

The Changing Face of Greece, Tamsin Osler, (Hodder Wayland)
What everyday life is like for people in Greece today

The Rough Guide to Greek, (Rough Guides)
A cheap, pocket-sized phrase book.

Wicked Websites

www.athens2004.com
The official website of the 2004 Olympic Games, with all the results of all the events

www.blueflag.org
Where to find Greece's cleanest beaches

www.culture.gr
The website of the Hellenic Ministry of Culture, no less, with lots of information on museums, monuments and historic sites, and what the Greeks think should happen to the Parthenon Marbles

www.epo.gr
The official wesbite of the Hellenic Football Federation, with plenty about Euro 2004 of course!

www.gnto.gr
The website of the Greek National Tourism Association, with lots of nice photos, useful maps and ideas for things to see when you're in Greece